STRATEGIC SUCCESS SERIES

FINANCIAL MANAGEMENT FOR NON-FINANCIAL MANAGERS

CLIVE MARSH

KoganPage

First published in Great Britain and the United States in 2012 by Kogan Page Limited

120 Pentonville Road	1518 Walnut Street, Suite 1100	4737/23 Ansari Road
London N1 9JN	Philadelphia PA 19102	Daryaganj
United Kingdom	USA	New Delhi 110002
www.koganpage.com		India

ISBN   978 0 7494 6467 7
E-ISBN   978 0 7494 6468 4

British Library Cataloguing-in-Publication Data

A CIP record for this book is available from the British Library.

Library of Congress Cataloging-in-Publication Data

Marsh, Clive (Clive Mark Heath)
   Financial management for non-financial managers / Clive Marsh.
      p. cm.
   Includes bibliographical references and index.
   ISBN 978-0-7494-6467-7 – ISBN 978-0-7494-6468-4 (ebook)
1. Business enterprises–Finance.   2. Corporations–Finance.   I. Title.
   HG4026.M3647 2012
   658.15–dc23

                                             2011043164

Typeset by Graphicraft Limited, Hong Kong
Printed and bound in India by Replika Press Pvt Ltd

CONTENTS

ONLINE RESOURCES

Additional resources to accompany the book are available on Kogan Page's *Strategic Success* website:

www.koganpage.com/strategicsuccess

Online template 1 – Departmental expenditure variance analysis
Online template 2 – Product contribution
Online template 3 – Cash forecast
Online template 4 – Planning and budgeting process
Online template 5 – Direct materials budget
Online template 6 – Direct labour budget
Online template 7 – Cost variance analysis – manufacturing

INTRODUCTION

As a manager your main task at all times is value creation and protection. You need to know where value comes from and how it is built or eroded. This requires a strategic understanding of financial management and managerial finance, and I hope that this little book will help you to become more financially literate. It is written for non-financial managers to improve their ability to evaluate the financial consequences of their decisions. Integrating finance and corporate strategy will help you and your finance director get a better understanding of how you both contribute to value creation.

The purpose of this book

The purpose of this book is to help non-financial managers understand finance and accounting at a managerial rather than a technical or professional level. This will help them make better decisions and manage their financial responsibilities more efficiently. At a strategic level it will help managers understand how financial strategy is integrated with business strategy. This is not a book aimed at financial experts or academics whose task is to explore new theories. It is a book for the practising business manager who needs practical and useful guidance on corporate finance and accounting.

Money is the common denominator of all business transactions, and accountancy provides a language and a method for recording the movements of money. A successful manager needs to have a strategic understanding of finance and accounting and also to understand how finance supports business strategy. Too much financial information can lead to complexity and confusion. This work will enable a manager to question the validity of information received and to concentrate on those financial performance indicators that are key to his/her business.

This work will also explain how different types of finance relate to various business structures, the role of accounting and finance departments, the analysis of financial statements, planning, budgeting, costing, pricing, investment appraisal, finance, taxation and international transactions. You will agree that this is a broad remit for such a short book and I must, therefore, cover the subjects at a high level only. However, this book will enable non-financial managers to feel confident when talking 'finance' with their finance directors, to manage their own financial responsibilities and to gain a better understanding of risk and the financial consequences of their actions.

After reading this book you will have a strategic understanding of:

- how to implement the controls required to protect financial assets;
- how to make sound strategic financial decisions;
- how to plan for and obtain funds;
- how to ensure that assets are used efficiently.

Strategic financial management creates real value within an organization, and this book will enable non-financial managers make sound financial decisions that add value. It is intended to bring together some of the most important financial principles and techniques in a way that will be useful to the practising manager. A key feature of this book is the provision of case studies in the final chapter that demonstrate the practical use and relevance of corporate financial management techniques.

It is expected that this book will be used by managers in different countries with different laws. Accordingly it has been written in a broad generic manner that outlines the general principles that are normal to most jurisdictions and regimes. It does not provide a strict legal or taxation framework. Any rates used are for illustrative purposes only and do not reflect actual rates.

The author

Clive Marsh is an experienced accountant, chief finance officer, corporate banker and business development director. He has worked for Shell, IBM, Cap Gemini, Ernst & Young and several corporate banks in the UK and overseas. He has also worked with a number of small and medium-sized businesses. His work has been published internationally.

Clive has a Masters' degree in strategic financial management from the Business School of Kingston University, London, is a member of the Institute of Chartered Accountants of New Zealand (ACA NZ), a fellow of the Chartered Bankers' Institute (FCIBS), a chartered banker and a fellow of the Chartered Management Institute.

CHAPTER ONE

TYPES OF BUSINESS STRUCTURE AND THEIR FINANCE

The aim of this chapter is to discuss the principal types of business entity and how they may raise initial capital.

Although there are many types of organization, for the purpose of this book, we will consider just three groups:

- *Sole proprietorships*: These are businesses that are owned by one person. They are generally small businesses. The owner of the business will have unlimited liability for the debts of the business and may even have to sell his/her home to clear the business debts if things go wrong. The capital for this type of business will be provided by the owner and finance may also be provided by way of loans, usually from a bank.
- *Partnerships*: These are businesses that are owned by two or more people who provide the capital. There are three principal types of partnership:
  - General partnerships: where the partners are jointly and severally liable for the debts of the partnership.
  - Limited partnerships: where there are one or more general partners and one or more limited partners whose liability is limited to a specified sum.
  - Limited liability partnerships (LLP): where the partners have limited liability. A partner in a LLP is not liable for another partner's misconduct or negligence.

  Partnerships may also obtain finance from banks and other lending institutions.

A disadvantage of a general partnership is that a partner may have to pay all partnerships debts if other partners or a partner are unable to do so.

- *Corporations*: These are limited liability businesses that have a separate legal personality from their owners (shareholders). In the event of the company winding up, the shareholders' liability will be limited. There are private limited companies and public limited companies. There are also other types of corporation but these are outside the scope of this book.

A major advantage of a limited liability company is the limit placed on a shareholder's liability in the event that the company folds.

There are advantages and disadvantages to each type of organization and the type of organization will have a bearing on the methods of finance adopted and on accounting and taxation. The advantages and disadvantages of the three principal types of organization are discussed below.

Sole proprietors

Some advantages of being a sole trader

- It is quick and easy to set up as a sole trader.
- The accounting is relatively simple.
- Simplicity. Less accountability.

Some disadvantages of being a sole trader

- There is no limit to the liability of the proprietor. The proprietor will be held personally liable for all debts in full and may have to use personal assets to clear off business debts.
- Sole traders have less ability to raise funds/capital.

As a sole trader you will be the initial provider of capital, unlike a partnership where partners contribute to capital or a company where the shareholders provide capital. So it will be harder to raise additional capital. Because a sole-trader business generally has less capital there will also be a reduced ability to borrow money since there is less 'equity' in the business. However, the great advantage of being a sole trader is that you are answerable primarily to yourself. There is no need to hold partner or shareholder meetings and prepare so many reports. This means that more time can be devoted to the business and direct income-earning activities.

A sole trader should keep separate accounts and have a separate bank account for the business so that there can be no confusion between your personal and non-business transactions. This will also make completing your tax returns easier.

As a sole trader you also need to make sure that the tax authorities cannot mistake you for an employee of your customer. This is especially the case if you have few customers. To do this it is important that you can be seen to be working for more than one customer, have your own tools/equipment, are in control of what you do and are able to hire others to do the work.

Banks like to see that a business has a reasonable amount of its own capital before they will lend, and will only lend up to a limit against this equity. This is the same as when you seek a mortgage on a house, where the bank likes you to have some equity. For this reason sole traders are not usually suitable business models for capital-intensive businesses that require large sums invested in plant and equipment.

There may be taxation disadvantages in being a sole trader compared with operating as a limited company or corporation. For example, the rate of taxation for individuals (sole traders) might be higher than the tax rate for corporations. Also, the timing of payments of tax may be different. Tax rules and rates obviously very from one country to another and you will need to seek advice about this from an accountant in your country of operation.

Partnerships: general and limited liability

A partnership has been described as 'the relationship which subsists between persons carrying on business in common with a view to profit'. It is brought into existence through the agreement of the parties concerned to carry on business for profit. Usually there will be a partnership agreement that sets out the rights, duties and responsibilities of the partners. This will include details of the capital of the partnership and the amount to be contributed by each of the partners. Other items included in the agreement will include partners' salaries (if any), interest to be allowed or charged to partners on loans or advances, and provisions for accounts, audits and so on.

Some of the principal advantages of a partnership

- It is usually possible to raise more capital than a sole trader can.
- There are various types of partnerships, including limited liability partnerships.
- Partners may bring additional skills, contacts and knowledge.
- The accounting and reporting might be a little simpler than for a company.

Some of the principal disadvantages of a partnership

- Partners may be held jointly and severally liable for the partnership debts. For example, if one partner fails to pay, the other partners may have to pay the failed partner's share.
- The partnership has to be dissolved when a partner dies, becomes bankrupt or leaves the partnership.
- A partnership agreement needs careful drafting.

Some countries place restrictions on the number of partners allowed in a partnership, although there may be exemptions for certain types of business. If you decide that a partnership is the most appropriate type of business structure then it is best to consult a lawyer who can advise you of any constraints and help draft a partnership agreement. At this stage you will also need to decide upon the type of partnership that is best for your business.

A general partnership will only have 'general members', where each partner is involved in the management and running of the partnership and takes responsibility for the liabilities of the firm, becoming both jointly and severally liable. This might be a real concern for some potential partners and would deter them from entering into such a partnership. To get round this it is possible to form a limited partnership whereby some members have their liability limited to a certain amount. This type of partnership will have both general and limited partners. Often the limited partners do not participate in the management of the firm.

In recent years a third category of partnership has become popular, particularly with accounting and other professional firms. This is the limited liability partnership (LLP), which combines characteristics of partnerships and corporations. An LLP is different from a general or a limited partnership. In an LLP all partners enjoy limited liability and are not responsible for any malpractice, incompetence or mistakes of others. They are, of course, responsible for their own acts.

Because a partnership will generally have access to more funds than a sole trader, it will be in a stronger position to raise loan finance from a bank.

Corporations

There are various types of corporation and for the purpose of this book we will discuss the principal ones.

A corporation is an entity in its own right, having its own legal existence separate from that of its members (owners). This means that when a member dies or sells his/her shares the company continues to exist regardless. This is quite different from a partnership or sole trader, which does not have the same separate legal existence.

A company limited by shares

A limited company is a type of corporation. The shareholders of a limited company own the company collectively and enjoy limited liability. This means that their liability towards the company's debts is limited to the amount, if any, unpaid on the shares taken up by them. Once the capital is fully paid there is no further liability on the shareholders. A company may be a private or a public company.

Limited companies

A private limited company is one that restricts the right to transfer shares and may limit the number of members. Shares may not be offered to the general public and shareholders may be bound to offer their shares to their fellow shareholders before offering them to a third party. Specific rules and terminology vary from country to country but this is the general principle. A private limited company will raise capital through the issue of shares and should be able to raise more funds than either a sole trader or a partnership.

Public limited companies

A public limited company (PLC) has shares that are traded to the public on a stock exchange. A PLC will have to comply with greater reporting and regulatory requirements than a private one, and with significant stock exchange regulations. PLCs are generally able to raise more funds than sole traders, partnerships or private limited companies. However, the reporting and regulatory demands on them can be burdensome for smaller companies and for this reason some small PLCs have reverted back to being private companies.

Summary

In this chapter we have discussed the principal types of business entity and how they may raise initial capital. In summary these are listed below:

- *Sole trader*: unlimited liability; initial funds from proprietor; limited ability to raise capital; simplicity; may be tax disadvantages depending on country of operation.
- *General partnerships*: may be liable for other partners' share of debts; initial funds from partners; relatively simple.
- *Limited partnerships*: some partners have limited liability; initial funds from partners.
- *Limited liability partnerships (LLPs)*: partners have limited liability; initial funds from partners.
- *Private limited company*: limited liability for members; initial funds from members; ability to raise more funds.
- *Public limited companies (PLCs)*: limited liability for members; initial funds from public members; possible to raise high levels of funds/capital.

Choosing the correct type of business structure is a primary strategic decision that will affect funding opportunities and the potential for future growth. All businesses require sound governance; however, as a general rule, the more stakeholders and more complexity in a business structure, the more attention will need to be paid to governance issues and processes.

CHAPTER TWO

THE ROLE OF THE ACCOUNTING AND FINANCE DEPARTMENT

Financial accounting, payroll, budgeting, management accounting, taxation, treasury

The aim of this chapter is to describe the role of the accounting and finance department and how it fits into an organization's structure.

No business can operate without an efficient supply of finance. It is the lifeblood of all organizations and the common denominator by which most business performance is measured both internally and externally. The accounting and finance department is at the centre of any organization and is responsible for ensuring the efficient financial management and financial controls necessary to support all business activities.

A good finance director needs to understand every aspect of a business so that s/he can develop a financial strategy that will support the business goals. Likewise, as a non-financial manager, it will help you become more effective in your own role if you have an understanding of the various roles of your organization's accounting and finance department.

The principal roles of the accounting and finance department, under the overall control of the finance director, can be conveniently grouped into:

- financial accounting;
- financial systems;
- payroll;
- budgeting;
- management accounting;
- taxation;
- treasury and financial planning;
- supporting the business strategy;
- creating value.

Financial accounting

This is concerned with keeping account of all transactions, using the double entry bookkeeping system and preparing final accounts suitable for meeting the various regulatory requirements for statutory reporting, the stock exchange and taxation authorities. The person responsible for this function in most medium to large organizations is the financial accountant, who will normally report to the finance director. Specific responsibilities of the financial accountant include:

- the recording of all transactions, using the double entry system;
- the maintenance of all ledgers, including purchases, sales and nominal ledgers;
- maintenance of the cash book and reconciliation of bank accounts;
- reconciliation of all accounts;
- preparation of accruals and prepayment entries in the accounts;
- keeping a fixed asset registers;
- debtors' control, debt collection and customer relations;
- creditor relations and supplier payments;
- stock reconciliations;
- recording of value added tax or similar taxes such as goods and services tax;
- completion of tax returns;
- extraction of a trial balance;
- preparation of final accounts, including a profit-and-loss account, balance sheet and funds statements;
- liaison with auditors and with taxation authorities;
- all external financial reporting;
- day-to-day banking relationships.

Financial systems

Medium- to large-sized organizations may employ a systems accountant, who will analyse the financial information needs of an organization and review existing systems. S/he is responsible for the design and maintenance of financial systems and for providing an interface between the finance and technology/systems departments. Within the accounting and finance function a systems accountant may report to the financial accountant, management accountant or financial director.

Systems accountants are involved in the implementation of change processes within the finance department and may manage new financial systems projects. They may also be required to assist other users of financial information.

Payroll

Larger organizations will have a paymaster or payroll manager. In smaller companies this task may be performed by the financial accountant. The payroll department is responsible for the following functions:

- liaison with taxation authorities to ensure that employer and employee details are correct and that taxes deducted are paid;
- receiving tax code notices and applying the correct tax code for each employee;
- completing returns to the taxation authorities;
- receiving timesheets and clock cards;
- ensuring basic pay, overtime and bonuses are calculated, recorded and paid and that deductions for taxes and pensions are made;
- ensuring employees are paid on time, using payment systems such as BACS or other methods;
- reconciling payroll accounts;
- providing advice to employees and the company.

Budgeting

In a larger organization budgeting may be carried out by a budget accountant. In a medium-sized company it may be undertaken by the management accountant.

Budgeting is concerned with the financial evaluation of plans and with reporting against this, normally on a monthly basis. Budgeting may include the following activities:

- helping managers prepare and evaluate their plans;
- preparing departmental budgets and consolidating them into a company budget;
- preparing an operating budget and a capital budget;
- obtaining approval for budgets;
- preparing reports that compare actual expenditures against budgets;
- analysing variances and seeking explanations;
- liaison with the financial accountant and the treasury manager.

Management accounting

Management accounting is concerned with the analysis and control of financial information to assist in the day-to-day operations of an organization. Most medium- to large-sized companies will have a management accountant responsible for this function who will report to the financial director. Management accounting includes, but is not limited to, the following activities:

- investment opportunity appraisal;
- cost and revenue estimates;
- budgeting as described above;
- analysis and decision making;
- capital investment decisions;
- management controls over the efficient use of resources;
- financial analysis.

Management accounting and financial accounting overlap in that management accounting reports are often based upon information derived from the financial accounting records. For example, the 'actual' expenditure figures shown in management accounts will be taken from the financial accounting records. Sometimes financial accounting and management accounting are integrated. An example of this would be the fully integrated standard costing system where the financial accounts are structured in such a way as to provide cost and management information directly.

Taxation

Most large companies will have a taxation department dealing with all tax affairs. In a smaller company this may be handled by the finance director or possibly the financial accountant.

As well as day-to-day taxation management and reporting, all decisions made by a company will have tax implications and these need to be identified and built into the decision-making process and financial plans. Not only does tax have to be accounted for but cash needs to be made available at the right time to pay it to the authorities. Tax does, therefore, affect cash planning and budgets.

Tax evasion is illegal and, in addition, most countries also have anti-avoidance laws. It is the tax department's responsibility to ensure that all laws are complied with. A brief list of the tax manager's duties includes:

- tax planning;
- understanding the taxation implications of decisions, trade and investments;
- double-taxation treaties;
- transfer pricing;
- direct taxation;
- company or corporation taxes;
- profit taxes;
- income taxes including Pay As You Earn (PAYE);
- capital gains tax;
- indirect taxation;
- VAT, goods and services tax, sales taxes;
- managing relations with taxation authorities.

There are many aspects of taxation that are open to debate and argument. This is why it is important to understand the taxation implications of business plans. Some companies adopt a more aggressive stance than others when dealing with a taxation authority. Others, often large multinational companies that value global relationships at a government level, may want to be seen as responsible tax citizens and adopt a more conciliatory approach. A large multinational company will have tax managers, some of whom are accountants and others who are lawyers specializing in taxation. Counsel's opinion will also be sought on aspects of tax law that are unclear.

Treasury and financial planning

Large corporations will have a treasurer with responsibility for the treasury function. The treasurer will normally report to the financial director. The treasurer is responsible for the efficient provision, investment and use of funds. Treasury responsibilities will include:

- cash management on a day-to-day basis;
- medium- and long-term cash planning;
- liquidity risk management to avoid running out of cash;
- interest rate risk management;
- foreign exchange risk management and understanding exposures;
- foreign exchange dealing – buying and selling currency;
- using derivatives, futures and swaps to help hedge against exposures;
- issuing debt;
- share issuance and capital structure;
- managing relationships with corporate and business bankers.

Supporting the business strategy

The finance director is a member of the executive team and is responsible for providing a financial environment that supports the business strategy. The right mix of short-term and long-term finance and equity funds needs to be available to meet the organization's aspirations and to provide the organizational agility needed to benefit from future opportunities. All managers have a primary responsibility to create value, and a primary responsibility of the finance director is to enable them to do this. Accordingly, financial strategy must first and foremost be integrated with the business plan.

Creating value

Within the context of the business plan the finance director has a responsibility to create value. This can be done through, for example, obtaining the best possible borrowing rates, cutting/controlling costs, reducing financial risks, improving debt collection, better cash management and many other activities that are discussed later in this book.

The 'mechanics' of these roles will be explained in more detail in the following chapters.

Accounting and finance department relationships

The accounting and finance department manage a number of internal and external relationships. These are detailed in Figure 2.1 below. Figure 2.2 shows the organization of a typical finance department.

FIGURE 2.1 Accounting and finance department relationships

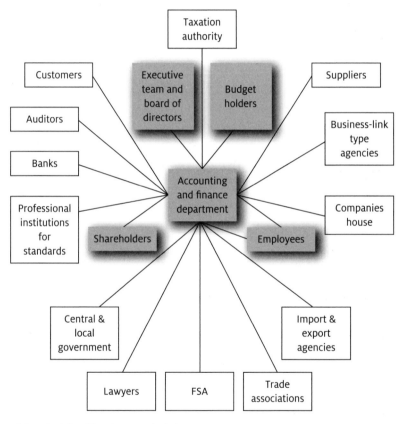

Internal relationships shown as shaded.

FIGURE 2.2 Organization of a typical finance department

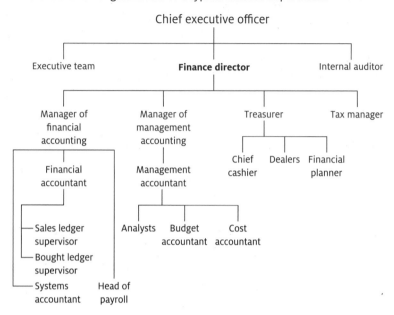

This chart shows the principal finance officers in a medium-sized organization. The number of staff reporting in through the principal officers will vary according to the size of operation and volume of transactions. In a small company the finance director often performs most of these functions him/herself often with just an assistant.

Summary

The finance director has overall responsibility for the accounting and finance department of an organization. He/she is a key member of an organization's senior management team and will be involved in all key decisions in addition to ensuring that day-to-day financial, legal and statutory requirements are met. The principal duties are: financial accounting, payroll, budgeting, management accounting, taxation, treasury and financial management. A primary responsibility is to ensure that the financial strategy is integrated with the overall business strategy, that there is adequate finance to support the business strategy and that the finance department adds value to the company.

CHAPTER THREE

ACCOUNTING AND FINANCIAL STATEMENTS

The purpose of this chapter is to provide a basic knowledge of the double entry system and of how accounts are constructed so as to enable you to understand financial statements and to make better decisions.

The basis for financial accounting is the double entry system. This system was first described in a work entitled *Summa de arithmetica, geometrica, proportioni et proportionali* compiled by the monk Luca Pacioli. It is a marvellous system that, if mastered, will make your understanding of financial management and business a whole lot easier.

The double entry system, like many good ideas, is very simple and it is my intention to enable you to grasp the basics that will help you understand financial statements. As this is a text for non-financial managers we will not be covering advanced financial accounting or international accounting standards and regulations. We will focus on the basics and what is generally accepted accounting practice throughout the world.

Double entry system and ledgers

The double entry system is so named because it recognizes that every financial transaction has two aspects: receiving and giving. So, if I were to receive €200 of cash from a customer I would record both aspects of the transaction in my accounts. I would show that I had received cash into my cash account and I would also show that my customer had paid me and record this in my customer accounts. Details of accounts are kept in ledgers that, of course, are now computerized. As another example, if I were to start a business with €100 I would record that the business now had €100 cash and that it owed me (the proprietor) €100.

So far so good?

Now here comes the tricky bit – the bit where some of you readers might think I have gone wrong!

To record the above €200 transaction I would make the following entries in my accounting system:

Debit	Cash Account	€200
Credit	Customer Account	€200

Note that I have debited my Cash Account with the €200 received and that I have credited my Customer Account with the €200 he has given. This is because under the <u>double entry system</u> you always:

- Debit the account that receives.

  &

- Credit the account that gives.

Now, I know what you might be thinking: this is different from what you expected because when you view a bank statement cash received is always shown on the statement as a credit. It is! But this is because when the bank receives a deposit from you it will debit its cash account and credit its customer's account (you) – just as I have done above. When you receive your bank statement it is a picture of the bank's account with you showing the credit. So, the bank operates the same system and performs the same entries as I have outlined above. Many people new to accounts struggle with this at first. However, you need to grasp this fundamental point before going any further. If you can understand and accept it the rest will be plain sailing!

Let's now look at some further examples:

Case 1

If a farmer buys a tractor for €25,000 from a dealer, the initial entries in the farmer's accounts will be:

| Debit | Asset (Tractor) | €25,000 |
| Credit | Dealer | €25,000 |

When the farmer actually pays the dealer, the entries in the farmer's accounts will be:

| Debit | Dealer | €25,000 |
| Credit | Cash | €25,000 |

Note that after this transaction is posted to the accounts the balance on the 'Dealer' account will be zero. This is because he has now been paid.

Case 2

If a business sells a service for €5,000 to a customer, the entries in the businesses accounts will be:

| Debit | Customer | €5,000 |
| Credit | Sales | €5,000 |

When the customer actually pays the business the €5,000, the entries in the businesses accounts will be:

| Debit | Cash | €5,000 |
| Credit | Customer | €5,000 |

Note that after this entry the balance on the 'Customer' account is zero. This is because the customer has now paid.

The above are basic examples showing how the double entry system works. In the example that follows you will see that:

● Accounts are debited with: assets, services received, expenses, losses.
● Accounts are credited with: payments made, services rendered, income and profit.

Example

Now work slowly through the following example showing basic accounting entries:

Tom, a sole trader, started business on 1 January 2012 as 'TJ Gardening'. To start the business he opened a business bank account and paid in €3,000 as the opening capital of the company. During the year ended 31 December 2012 the following transactions took place:

3000

20/1/12	Purchased plants 20 plants @ €10 each cash	€200
15/3/12	Sells 10 plants @ €90 each to Mr Brown	€900
14/4/12	Receives cash from Mr Brown	€900
16/6/12	Pays rent/rates/services	€800
18/8/12	Purchases plant and equipment with cash	€300
25/11/12	Charged depreciation* on plant and equipment	€100

*Plant and equipment have been used and depreciated in value.

Show all of the above entries in the accounts, take out a trial balance and prepare financial statements (profit-and-loss account and balance sheet) as at 31/12/12.

The entries to be posted in the accounts are:

1/1/12	Debit	Bank account	€3,000
1/1/12	Credit	Capital account	€3,000
20/1/12	Debit	Plants account	€200
20/1/12	Credit	Bank account	€200
15/3/12	Debit	Debtor, Mr Brown	€900
15/3/12	Credit	Sales	€900
15/3/12	Debit	Cost of sales (10×€10)	€100
15/3/12	Credit	Plants account	€100
14/4/12	Debit	Bank account	€900
14/4/12	Credit	Debtor, Mr Brown	€900
16/6/12	Debit	Rent/rates/power account	€800
16/6/12	Credit	Bank account	€800
18/8/12	Debit	Plant and equipment account	€300
18/8/12	Credit	Bank account	€300
25/11/12	Debit	Depreciation expenses account	€100
25/11/12	Credit	Depreciation provision account	€100

When you have understood the above entries see below how they are recorded in the accounts –/debits on the left and credits on the right:

		Debits			Credits
Bank Account:	1/1/12	Capital account	£3,000	20/1/12 Plants account	£200
	14/4/12	Mr Brown	£900	16/6/12 Rent/Rates/Power 18/8/12 Plant and equipment	£800 £300
Capital Account:				1/1/12 Bank account	£3,000
Plants Account:	20/1/12	Cash Account	£200	15/3/12 Cost of sales	£100
Cost of sales account:	15/3/12	Plant Account	£100		
Sales Account:				15/3/12 Mr Brown	£900
Debtors Account (Mr Brown):	15/3/12	Sales account	£900	14/4/12 Bank account	£900
Rent/Rates/Power Expense Account:	16/6/12	Bank account	£800		
Plant and equipment account:	18/8/12	Bank account	£300		
Depreciation Expenditure Account:	25/11/12	Depn. provision	£100		
Depreciation Provision Account:				25/11/12 Depn. Expenditure	£100

Follow the above entries one step at a time. Note that debit entries are always on the left and credits are on the right. This is the standard form. Note also that the corresponding entry is shown in each account description of the transaction. For the sake of simplicity I have not totalled the above accounts. There are few entries in this example and it is easy enough to see what the balance values are. For example, the balance of the cash account is €2,600 debit (cash in the bank).

We will now prepare a trial balance and you can see the balances of the accounts and this will also prove the arithmetic accuracy.

Trial balance .

Trial balance as at 31/12/12

Debit balances		Credit balances	
Cash	€2,600	Capital account	€3,000
Plants acount	€100	Sales acount	€900
Cost of sale account	€100	Depreciation povision	€100
Rent/Rates/Power Exp	€800		
Plant and equipment account	€300		
Depreciation expenses	€100		
Total debits	**€4,000**	**Total credits**	**€4,000**

The above trial balance is just a list of balances of all the accounts. It only provides proof of the arithmetical accuracy of the accounting entries. We can now use this to prepare the final accounts – a profit-and-loss account and a balance sheet.

Profit-and-loss account

Sales	900
Cost of sales	100
Gross profit margin	800
Rent/Rates/Power Expense	800
Depreciation expense	100
Net profit/(loss)	**(100)**

Note that the trader has actually made a loss during the first year of trading. He still has plenty of cash in the bank, but after all costs including depreciation he has made a loss.

The next stage is to prepare a balance sheet to show the overall financial position.

Balance sheet

Liabilities:		
Capital account	3,000	
Profit-and-loss account	(100)	
Proprietor's equity	**2,900**	
Assets:		
Fixed Assets:		
Plant and Equipment	300	
Less Depreciation Provision	(100) – 200	
Current Assets:		
Plant stock account	100	
Cash account	2,600 – 2,700	
Total Assets	**2,900**	

Notes to the accounts:

1 The accounts show a gross profit of €800. However, after expenses of €900 (€800+€100) the final result was a net loss of €100.
2 The proprietor's equity has been reduced to €2,900. This is because the initial equity/capital has been partially offset by the loss of €100 (€3,000–€100). Had the trader made a profit then his equity would have increased.

3 Note that proprietor's equity/capital is shown as a liability. This is because the business unit has a liability to the proprietor for the initial capital injected plus any retained profits or, in this case, less any losses.

4 Note that the value of fixed assets has been reduced by the depreciation provision.

We have shown above a simple profit-and-loss account and a balance sheet. A third type of financial statement you might see is a funds statement. This is simply a statement that shows where funds have been sourced from and how they have been applied. An example is given below.

The basic accounting equation is:

Equity = Assets less External Liabilities
(external liabilities include items such as creditors and bank loans)

In our case €2,900 = €2,900 − €0 (there being no external liabilities)

Classification of assets and liabilities

When reading financial statements you will note that assets and liabilities are classified into various categories. The usual classifications are listed below.

Fixed assets

These include items such as machinery, equipment, vehicles, buildings, furniture and other items of a permanent nature that will not be consumed within the accounting period. Of course, an asset may be used in the accounting period and may depreciate in value. This is why we allow for depreciation and reduce the value of an asset.

Current assets

These include cash or items that can be readily converted into cash such as debts or stock.

Assets are normally shown in the balance sheet at cost less any depreciation. It is not prudent to show them at a higher value that has/may not be realized. For example, stocks are normally shown at the lower of cost or net realizable value.

Long-term liabilities

These are liabilities (amounts owing by the business) that are not due for repayment within one year from the accounting date. Examples are equity and term loans.

Current liabilities

These are liabilities that are repayable immediately or within one year of the accounting date. Examples are bank overdrafts (repayable on demand) and trade creditors.

Summary of profit-and-loss account and balance sheet

The above example of a profit-and-loss account and balance sheet together with their underlying accounting entries is highly simplified and is designed to help your understanding of financial statements. We will cover the analysis of financial statements in the next chapter.

Profit-and-loss accounts and balance sheets are the basic financial statements. There is another statement that helps users of financial statements understand how funds have been sourced and applied. This is called a Source and Application of Funds Statement and is described briefly below.

Source and application of funds statements

The purpose of these statements is to show where a company has sourced its funds from and how it has applied them. Since funds statements are only concerned with items involving the movement of funds, depreciation is added back to net profits. This is best explained by an example shown in the table below.

	2012 £m	2011 £m
Sources of funds:		
Profit before tax	40.5	10.5
Depreciation (add back)	30.5	28.5
	71.0	39.0
Shares issued for cash	10.0	10.0
Proceeds from sale of assets	12.0	11.0
	93.0	**60.0**
Application of funds:		
Dividends paid	5.0	5.0
Taxes paid	15.0	10.0
Movement in working capital	5.0	5.0
	25.0	20.0
Movement in borrowing:	68.0	40.0
	93.0	**60.0**

This statement shows that during 2012 the company sourced €71.0m of funds from profits, €10.0m from a share issue and a further €12.0 million from selling off assets. This totalled €93m and this sum was applied to paying dividends and taxes, and to changes in working capital and borrowing balances. Some investors find this statement useful whilst others simply read the P&L and balance sheet. It is a useful statement in that it shows at a glance where funds have come from and where they have been used.

Principles: matching, accruals, deferrals, consistency, conservatism, accounting periods, materiality, going-concern concept, form and substance, full disclosure and clarity

There are some basic principles that need to be adhered to when preparing accounts. Some of the more fundamental ones are listed below.

Matching

This principle requires that expenditure of one period is matched with income of the same period.

An invoice may be paid in one financial year that relates to services spread over several years. For example an annual insurance premium paid on 30 September 2011 might relate to cover for three months in 2011 and nine months in 2012. It would be entirely wrong to charge all of the 2011 year with the total amount paid on 30 September 2011. Some of the charge should be deferred to the following year and matched with income of that year.

This is best explained by means of an example:

During the year ended 31 December 2013 sales were €30,000 and the cost of those sales was €18,000.

Rent was paid annually in advance on 30 June and was €4,000 in 2012 and €6,000 in 2013. What is the net profit for the year ended 31 December 2013?

Sales	€30,000
Cost of sales	€18,000
Gross profit	€12,000
Rent 1 January 2013 to 30 June 2013 is €4,000/2	€2,000
Rent 1 July 2013 to 31 December 2013 is €6,000/2	€3,000
Net profit	€7,000

Note that the rent applicable to 2013 and charged in the accounts was €5,000 and not the €6,000 that was actually paid. €2,000 of the rent actually paid in 2012 related to 2013 and only €3,000 of the rent paid in 2013 actually related to 2013. This is the concept of matching income and expenditure in the same accounting period. It is achieved through the accounting processes of accruals and deferrals, which are explained below.

Accruals

When a cost has been incurred but the invoice for it has not been received it will be necessary to accrue for the cost in the accounting period it was incurred. For example if electricity is invoiced quarterly in arrears then it will be necessary to read the amount of electricity used and estimate the value of this. An entry is made in the accounts to recognize this. For example, if it is estimated that €500 of electricity has been used but not invoiced then the accounting entry in the period it was used would be:

Debit	Electricity expenditure	€500
Credit	Accrued creditors	€500

This entry will ensure that the cost is taken up in the correct period and matched with income of that same period. It will also reflect an accrued liability in the balance sheet.

In the subsequent period when the actual invoice is received (let's assume it was for €510) then the entry in the accounts would be:

Debit	Accrued creditors	€500
Debit	Electricity expenditure	€10
Credit	Creditors	€510

The accrued creditors account will now have a zero balance, electricity expenditure for the new period will only be charged with €10 (being the underestimate) and creditors will show a balance of €510, as the actual amount owing to the electricity supply company.

Deferrals

Sometimes costs are paid in advance. For example, insurance premiums are often paid annually in advance. If this is the case then the amount paid in advance will need to be deferred to the next period in order to ensure that costs and income are matched.

Consistency

Transactions and valuations need to be treated in a consistent way in order to avoid confusing fluctuations in profit. A good example of this is in the case of stock valuations, where a change in the method of valuation such as the amount of overheads absorbed into stock/work in progress can have a dramatic effect on the level of profitability reported. For this reason valuation methods need to be consistently applied from one accounting period to the next. If it is necessary to change a method of valuation (for example) then the effect of this change must be clearly reported.

Conservatism

This means taking a cautious approach in calculating the level of profits. Bring in all costs as soon as they are incurred and recognized. Only recognize income when it is certain.

Accounting periods

Divide the business reporting up into consistent accounting periods, usually 12-month periods for annual accounts and six-month periods for interim accounts. Don't change periods so that comparisons become confusing. If it is essential to change periods, bring together different periods or report different periods, then full explanations need to be given and proper comparative statements need to be prepared. This may happen for a number of reasons such as a merger or a start up, and as a reader of accounts you will need to be aware that you will need to compare like with like periods.

Materiality

Don't worry too much if accounting mistakes are so small as to have no material effect on the overall impression that the accounts give. Of course, all mistakes need to be rectified but as a reader of financial statements you need to be aware of what is and is not material. A misstatement or omission is said to be material if it influences the overall view provided in the accounts.

Going-concern concept

The value of a business will depend upon whether or not it is considered to be a continuing going concern. A business that is folding will have a break-up value that is different from its going-concern value. This is an important concept in many ways. For example, the directors of a company must not take on more debt once they are aware that the company has ceased to be a going concern and will cease trading. Allowing a company to take on more debt when knowing that it is no longer a going concern is fraud.

Form and substance

This principle requires that financial statements should show the true view and not just the strict legal view.

Full disclosure and clarity

All relevant facts need to be disclosed in a clear way. Important facts must not be omitted and financial statements must not provide a mass of confusing information that hides important items that need to be disclosed.

These basic accounting principles have been applied to many types of business transaction and have formed the basis of detailed accounting standards that are published internationally. A detailed analysis of these accounting standards is beyond the scope of this book. However, if you are interested in finding out more, simply search for 'accounting standards' on your web browser and you will find that standards have been written to cover many accounting issues. The basic accounting principles discussed above have been incorporated into what are known as GAAP (Generally Accepted Accounting Principles).

Accounting and the environment

Accountants are increasingly recognizing their role in helping to provide information that enables people to understand the broader environmental and social consequences of organizational activity. Sustainability accounting is at varying stages of development throughout the world and there are developing tools that attempt to incorporate sustainability considerations into organizational decision making. Increasingly you may notice sustainability statements within conventional financial statements. These may include reports on:

- carbon emissions;
- social responsibility;
- environmental impacts;
- sustainability of operations.

The purpose of theses reports is to consider the impact of organizational activity on the broader external environment, economy and society.

Neuroscience and accounting

When you start to think in accounting terms you might find that business life becomes easier and more comfortable! Strange as it might seem, some academics believe that accounting may have evolved from the way the brain thinks about exchange opportunities. Emerging research suggests that the evolution of accounting practice can be traced to neuronal processes.

The assumption is that human economies are built on reciprocal exchanges and accounting concepts such as double entry, matching and conservatism are believed to be in harmony with the way the brain functions. An example is the concept of conservatism where gains are not anticipated but losses are. Neuroscience research suggests that the brain reacts differently to gains and losses. Brain scans have shown that areas of the brain that are related to reward and conflict resolution are activated more by losses than by gains. The findings show that subjects require 1.97 units of gain to compensate for 1 unit of loss.

These findings were published in the *Chartered Accountants Journal* (NZ) in May 2011 in an article by Steven Cahan, FCA. The article might help explain why accounting makes business easier. The article is based upon work published by J de Quervain, U Fishbacher, V Treyer, M Schellammer, U Schyder, A Buck, E Fehr, S Basu, J Dickhaut, G Hecht, K Towry, G Waymire, M Kirk, F Castelli, F Happe, U Frith, C Frith, K McCabe, S Toms, C Fox, C Trespel and R Poldrack.

Summary

As a non-financial manager it is unlikely that you will need a detailed technical knowledge of accounting or of the double entry system. It is most likely that you will be reading completed financial statements or attending to your departmental budget statements. However, having a basic knowledge of the double entry system and of how accounts are constructed will enable you to understand financial statements and to make better decisions.

In this chapter we have explained the basics of how accounts are prepared, including accounting entries, trial balances, profit-and-loss accounts and balance sheets. We have completed the chapter with an overview of important accounting principles.

In the chapters that follow we will learn how to interpret financial statements and manage finances. Underlying this will be the basics covered in this chapter, so it is important that you have understood it. Accountancy is, perhaps, like riding a bike in that it is easier learned than taught! Practice makes perfect and if you are having any doubts go through the chapter again and work through the examples.

This short chapter is based upon the Generally Accepted Accounting Principles of the UK. To bring countries into line with each other, international financial reporting standards have been developed. Details of these can now be searched on the web for those readers that have an interest.

CHAPTER FOUR

ANALYSIS AND FINANCIAL RATIOS

In the previous chapter we covered the basics of accounts preparation. We will now examine completed financial statements and show how they can be used to analyse performance. In this chapter we will cover the essential ratios that are used to provide a guide to business performance.

Below are examples of a typical profit-and-loss account (Table 4.1) and balance sheet (Table 4.2) for a medium-sized company. We will use these financial statements for further analysis. Read the accounts and become familiar with this layout. A full set of published accounts will contain considerably more information. However, the basic principles are the same. I have kept things simple so as not to confuse you with too much data.

We will now use these accounts to undertake a ratio analysis and compare the results of 2013 against 2012 in order to get a better understanding of how the company has performed. Shareholders, future investors, lenders and other stakeholders will use published accounts and ratio analysis to help make their decisions. Of course, the information in year-end accounts is largely out of date and they will also refer to interim accounts, management accounts and other information.

TABLE 4.1 Profit and loss account for X Ltd

	2013 £m	2012 £m
Sales	650	700
Cost of sales (materials)	300	340
Gross profit	350 (54%)	360 (51%)
Expenses	100	120
Profit before interest and taxation	250	240
Interest	30	40
Profit before taxation	220	200
Taxation	66	60
Profit after taxation	154	140
Dividends paid to shareholders	40	50
Profit retained	114	90

NOTE: Gross profit is sometimes referred to as gross margin. It is also often expressed as a percentage of sales and called the gross profit percentage or gross margin percentage. In our example for 2013 it is 54 per cent (350 as a percentage of 650).

Ratio analysis

Ratio analysis is a way of gaining a better understanding of financial performance. Ratios enable comparisons between periods and with other companies. They enable us to track efficiency and profitability. They can be used to reveal trends in profitability, efficiency, gearing, liquidity and returns on investment. In this chapter we will explain some of the more commonly used and, therefore, useful financial ratios.

TABLE 4.2 Balance sheet on X Ltd

	2013 £m	2012 £m
Fixed assets:		
Plant & equipment (after depreciation)	150	160
Current assets:		
Stock	200	250
Debtors	150	170
Cash at bank	50	60
Current liabilities:		
Trade creditors	(160)	(180)
Bank overdraft	(100)	(110)
Net current assets:	140	190
Total fixed and net current assets:	**290**	**350**
Capital & reserves:		
Called up share capital	150	150
Retained profits	140	26
Term loan	–	174
	290	**350**

Note that the company has been able to repay the term loan of £174m during the year by retaining profits of £114m and reducing total fixed and net current assets by £60m.

Gross profit percentage

This ratio is sometimes called the gross margin. It is probably the most widely used and quoted ratio. It shows the ratio of gross profit to sales expressed as a percentage.

In our example above for the year 2013 the gross profit was €350m and sales were €650m.

The gross profit percentage is:

$$\frac{\text{Gross profit}}{\text{Sales}} \times \frac{100}{1}$$

$$\frac{350\text{m}}{650\text{m}} \times \frac{100}{1}$$

Gross profit percentage = **54%**

This is an improvement on the previous year when the gross profit percentage was 51 per cent. An analyst would compare these gross profit percentages with those achieved in similar businesses.

The gross profit percentage is also a useful measure to compare the contribution that individual product sales make towards a company's overall fixed costs.

Net profit percentage

This ratio compares net profit to sales and is calculated as follows:

$$\frac{\text{Net profit}}{\text{Sales}} \times \frac{100}{1}$$

In the above example for X Ltd the net profit (after tax and interest) ratio for 2013 is:

$$\frac{154}{650} \times \frac{100}{1}$$

Net profit percentage = **24 per cent**

This ratio indicates that the net profit after interest and taxation is 24 per cent of sales.

Another net profit ratio often quoted by analysts is Net Profit Before Interest & Taxation (NBIT).

There are a number of variations used by analysts when quoting net profit ratios and you need to be sure that you understand what an analyst has used so that you can compare like with like.

Current ratio

This ratio measures the solvency of a business by comparing current assets with current liabilities. It is normally shown just as a single figure.

$$\text{Current ratio} = \frac{\text{Current assets}}{\text{Current liabilities}}$$

Table 4.3 measures the ratio using figures from the balance sheet of X Ltd for 2013. Since this is a positive number it indicates that on a going-concern basis the company is solvent. However, the company does have to collect its debts and convert its stock into sales and ultimately cash in order to be able to pay its creditors. Remember also that bank over-drafts are repayable on demand. There is a stricter test of a company's actual liquidity rather than just its solvency; this is called the liquidity ratio, which is explained below.

TABLE 4.3 Ratios for X Ltd

Stock and work in progress	200
Debtors	150
Cash at bank	50
Total current assets	400
Trade creditors	(160)
Bank overdraft	(100)
Total current liabilities	(260)
Current ratio =	400
	‾‾‾‾
	260
Current ratio =	**1.54**

Liquidity ratio

The liquidity ratio indicates a company's ability to repay its debts as they fall due. It is usually expressed as a single figure. A figure that is greater than '1' would indicate that the company is liquid. A ratio of less than '1' would indicate that the company might struggle to pay debts when they are due.

$$\text{Liquidity ratio} = \frac{\text{Liquid assets}}{\text{Current liabilities}}$$

Liquid assets are cash and debtors. Stock is not a liquid asset since it still has to be converted into a sale.

In our example for X Ltd the liquidity ratio for 2013 is:

$$\text{Liquidity ratio} = \frac{150 + 50}{260}$$

Since this liquidity ratio is less than one, it might indicate that the company could have problems in repaying debts as they fall due. It will certainly need to ensure that it collects cash from its own debtors before it can pay all of its creditors. Although this company appears to be profitable it does need to ensure that it does not 'overtrade' and find itself without enough liquidity. Perhaps it needs to convert some of its stock more quickly into sales and reduce stock levels even further.

This ratio is useful in highlighting areas for management attention.

Stock-turnover ratio

This ratio measures how fast stock moves through a business. Holding on to stock is expensive, since there is an interest cost on funds invested in stock and there are also holding costs such as warehousing and storage. Also, stock may degrade if held for too long. Conversely, it might be beneficial to buy stocks early at a time of rising prices and also to take advantage of any quantity discounts by purchasing greater quantities than are immediately needed by the production department. If stock levels are kept too low then there might be a chance of not having material required to meet production schedules or to make up customer orders. There is an optimal level of stock that needs to be held and this requires careful calculation.

The stock-turnover ratio is just a simple measure of how quickly stock moves and a high stock-turnover number would generally be considered healthy since fewer funds were being tied up in stock. Be aware that stock-turnover ratios calculated using year-end figures can be concealing significant movements during the accounting period. In other words, the year-end value of stock may not reflect average stock values. This consideration also applies to other ratios that have been calculated using year-end values. The calculation for stock turnover usually uses average stock values.

$$\text{Stock turnover} = \frac{\text{Cost of sales (material costs only)}}{\text{Average stock values}}$$

The average stock value can be calculated in the case of X Ltd by using the opening and closing values of stock and dividing them by 2.

$$\text{Average stock} = \frac{200 + 250}{2}$$

$$\text{Average stock} = 225$$

$$\text{Stock turnover} = \frac{300 \text{ (cost of sales, materials)}}{225 \text{ (material cost)}}$$

Stock turnover = **1.33 times p.a.**

This is a slow rate of stock turnover. It may well be necessary in this type of business. However, it is not good for liquidity, as indicated in the liquidity ratio previously mentioned. It means that the company will need to ensure it has sufficient funds to invest in stock and is aware of the significant stock holding cost.

Debtors' days

Debtors' days is an indication of how good a company is at collecting debts from its customers and how much trade credit it allows. The fewer days the better.

The calculation for debtor days is:

$$\text{Debtors' days} = \frac{\text{Debtors} \times 365}{\text{Sales}}$$

In the case of X Ltd for 2013:

$$\text{Debtors' days} = \frac{150 \times 365}{650}$$

$$\text{Debtors' days} = \textbf{84 days}$$

Again, this would not generally be considered a good sign since 84 days is slow. Of course, it depends upon the business. For example a car repair business may have debtors' days of just five whilst an undertaker may consider 90 days to be normal.

Average balances can be used to calculate debtors' days. Also, it is often more helpful to show the value of debtors falling into different period categories, such as 0–30 days, 31–60 days, 61–90 days and over 90 days.

It can now be seen that the poor liquidity ratio of company X Ltd is mainly caused by poor debt collection and a poor stock turnover as indicated in the ratios.

Fixed assets turnover ratio

This measures the efficiency of fixed asset usage by comparing fixed assets with sales. It is calculated as follows:

$$\text{Fixed assets turnover ratio} = \frac{\text{Sales turnover}}{\text{Fixed assets}}$$

In the case of X Ltd this will be:

$$\text{Fixed assets turnover ratio} = \frac{650}{150}$$

$$\text{Fixed assets turnover ratio} = \textbf{4 times p.a.}$$

This is one ratio that varies enormously depending on the type of business. For example a manufacturing company with heavy plant and equipment may have a greater fixed asset value than a marketing agency with a similar sales turnover. Again, it is useful to use average fixed asset values rather than end-of-year balances.

Gearing ratio

This important ratio shows the level of a company's external borrowing compared with its equity (shareholders' funds). A company is said to be highly geared when it has a high level of external borrowing compared to equity. One way of expressing gearing is as a simple percentage as follows:

$$Gearing = \frac{External\ loans}{Internal\ equity}$$

Assuming a company has bank loans outstanding of €700,000 and shareholders' funds (called up capital and retained earnings) of €3,500,000 then the gearing ratio will be:

$$Gearing\ ratio = \frac{700,000}{3,500,000}$$

Gearing ratio = **20 per cent**

This result will generally be considered as healthy and as a lowly geared company. As with other ratios it all depends on the type of business.

In our example we have shown gearing as the ratio of loans to equity. Some analysts may show it other ways. For example, they may show gearing as the ratio of loan capital to total capital (loans + equity). When comparing gearing ratios, always be sure that you are comparing ratios using the same methods/formulas. Gearing may also be calculated using market values. For the purpose of clarity I am sticking with the basic method that demonstrates the principle of gearing.

Return on capital employed ratio

The return on equity ratio is often referred to as ROCE. This ratio compares profits with the capital employed to earn the profits.

$$ROCE\ per\ cent = \frac{Profit\ before\ interest\ \&\ tax}{Capital\ employed}$$

There are various definitions for capital employed. Often it is defined as shareholders' funds plus term loans.

Example: If a company makes a profit before interest and tax of €250,000 when shareholders' funds were €500,000 and term loans were €100,000 then the ROCE would be:

$$ROCE = \frac{250,000}{500,000 + 100,000}$$

ROCE = **42 per cent**

This means that for every €1 of capital employed in the company there is a profit (before interest and tax) of €0.42

Return on equity: earnings per share

The return on equity (ROE) ratio shows the rate of return achieved by the equity investors in a company. It is expressed as the percentage of profit before interest and tax (PBIT) is to equity.

$$ROE = \frac{PBIT}{Equity}$$

In the case of X Ltd for the year ended 2013 this would be:

$$ROE = \frac{250}{290}$$

ROE = **86 per cent**

Earnings per share (EPS)

This is the amount of earnings attributable to each equity share. For example, if a company has paid up capital of 100,000 ordinary shares of €5 and makes a net profit after tax of €50,000 then the earnings per share will equal 50 cents per share. Simply divide the net profit after tax by the number of shares.

$$Earnings\ per\ share\ (EPS) = \frac{Net\ profit\ after\ tax}{Number\ of\ ordinary\ shares}$$

$$EPS = \frac{€50,000}{100,000}$$

EPS = **€0.50 per share**

The price–earnings ratio (PER)

The purpose of this ratio is to compare the actual earnings per share with the market price of one ordinary share.

$$PER = \frac{\text{Market price of ordinary share}}{\text{Earnings per share (EPS)}}$$

Assuming the market price of the above shares is €6 and that the earnings per share are 50 cents then the price–earnings ratio would be:

$$PER = \frac{6.00}{0.50}$$

$$PER = 12$$

The PER shows the relationship between return and market price and is, therefore, of importance to investors and the market.

Earnings–yield

This is another way of expressing the price–earnings ratio (PER).

$$\text{Earnings–yield} = \frac{\text{EPS}}{\text{Share price}} \times \frac{100}{1}$$

Using the above figures:

$$\text{Earnings–yield} = \frac{0.50}{6.00} \times \frac{100}{1}$$

$$\text{Earnings–yield} = \textbf{8.3 per cent}$$

Dividend cover

This shows us how many times a dividend could have been paid from earnings. It is measured as a number and the higher the number the better the cover.

$$\text{Dividend cover} = \frac{\text{Earnings per share}}{\text{Dividend per share}}$$

If a company has earnings per share of 50 cents and pays a dividend of 10 cents on each share then the dividend cover will be five times.

$$\text{Dividend cover} = \frac{50}{10}$$

Dividend cover = **5 times**

Dividend yield

The dividend yield shows the dividend return against the market value of an investment.

$$\text{Dividend yield} = \frac{\text{Dividend}}{\text{Share price}} \times \frac{100}{1}$$

If a dividend of 10 cents is paid when the market price of a share is €6, the dividend yield will be:

$$\text{Dividend yield} = \frac{0.10}{6.00} \times \frac{100}{1}$$

Dividend yield = **1.7 per cent**

Summary

Ratio analysis is a useful tool. It draws attention to areas that need further examination and explanations. You will have noticed that in this chapter I have used words such as 'generally', 'usually' and 'depending'. This is because we need to take care not to jump to conclusions when using ratio analysis. It is a tool to guide our questioning and for further analysis. Don't jump in and make the wrong diagnosis!

You may also have noticed that ratios are connected to each other. Some professional analysts like to link ratios together using a method called the Du Pont system. The value of this is that, given only a certain amount of information, it might be possible to obtain a fuller picture by deduction. The detail of this method is beyond the scope of this text but if you are interested then you can explore this initially on the web.

In this chapter we have covered the essential ratios that are used to provide a guide to business performance. At this stage you should know:

- how accounts are prepared using the double entry system;
- understand the basic layout of a profit-and-loss account and balance sheet;
- be able to analyse accounts and ask pertinent questions using ratio analysis as a base.

Ratio analysis can become addictive, in that once you have become proficient you might find yourself comparing and analysing accounts whenever they are published. This is good practice and will enable you to make comparisons between companies and seek answers. For example, if you notice that two companies selling the same product have very different gross margins, ask why this should be. Is there a difference in scale of operations? Do the companies operate in different markets? Is there a difference in the quality of what appear to be similar products? Is one company more efficient than the other? Is there a difference in brand strength? This type of approach will enable you to gain a better understanding of the industry sector and help you make better executive decisions.

CHAPTER FIVE

PLANNING AND BUDGETING

In this chapter we will explain how departmental budgets are prepared from plans and how performance against them is monitored. A budget should be the financial evaluation of a plan. Accordingly the budget process follows on from an initial business plan. It is also part of a planning process because once the financial consequences of a plan of action are known the plan may need to be revised.

The planning and budgeting process shown in Figure 5.1 demonstrates how budgeting needs to be integrated with the planning process. As far as possible budgets should be zero-based. Zero-based budgets (ZBB) assume that each year the budget holder starts from scratch and has to justify each item of expenditure to support the operational strategy, key tasks and goals. Some budgets will be dependent upon other budgets. For example, a production budget may be dependent upon a sales budget. A budget for new plant and equipment (a capital budget) might be dependent upon the requirements of production. Each business will have its own budgeting hierarchy and budget dependencies. However, typical planning and budgeting dependencies are shown in Figure 5.2.

The planning and budgeting process

FIGURE 5.1 A planning and budgeting process

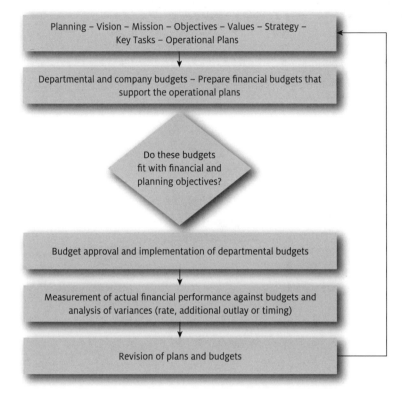

This illustration shows how certain budgets depend upon the completion of other budgets and that all budgets must support the overall organizational goals and operational strategy. The marketing plan and strategy will help kick off the sales budget, which in turn will form a basis for a production budget and a debtors budget. The production budget will help budget for creditors and stocks, and also identify plant and equipment (capital budget). This will form the budget for depreciation and also help identify any long-term funding. Departmental overhead budgets to support sales and production will be completed and budgets that affect cash flow will feed into the cash budget. Budgets affecting the profit-and-loss and balance sheet budgets will help the

FIGURE 5.2 Budget dependencies

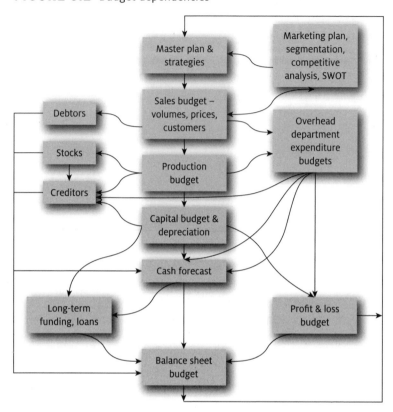

accountant complete a forecast financial position and this will then be fed back into the high-level planning process to see if the evaluated plans (budgets) are feasible. Plans and budgets are continually adjusted by budget holders and executive teams as new information comes to light and this is why a budgeting process will usually take some months to complete.

Much of what we have discussed so far will not be the responsibility of the non-financial manager but will be undertaken by the accountant or financial director. However, having an understanding of the whole process will enable you to get a better understanding of your company's planning and budgeting cycle.

Departmental budgets and variance analysis

Possibly of more importance to you will be your own departmental budget for operating costs and for capital equipment. Operating costs are items such as salaries, rent, power, stationery, advertising, travel and accommodation, whilst capital equipment costs are for fixed assets such as plant, equipment, vehicles and furniture.

The first stage in a departmental budget is to estimate what resources your department needs to achieve the goals and key tasks that have been agreed as part of the overall planning process. In doing this you might want to consider what was spent in the previous year in order to get a feel for the cost of certain items. However, you should most definitely not simply take last year's actual costs and repeat them as the current year budget because this would not reflect zero-based budgeting! An allowance must also be made for inflation.

Key budgets: sales, production, materials, labour, overheads, capital

A departmental work sheet for the finance department's operating budget could look like the one shown in Table 5.1.

Note that each item in the budget is related to a key task. Key tasks flow from the operational strategy and are usually given numbers. For example, Key Task Number 3 could be: 'to meet company statutory and legal obligations'. Some companies may call them key tasks but use some other term. The point here is to remember that you will need to justify your expenditure and link it back to the overall organizational plan. Your accountant should prepare a working sheet that helps you do this.

The 2012 column is for the previous year and is used as a guide only, to see if costs are reasonable for undertaking a similar key task. It can also be helpful to ensure that items are not omitted.

The accountant will feed your figures into the overall consolidated company budgets that show overall salaries, stationery costs and so on. S/he should also consolidate the costs of undertaking key tasks.

The cost of achieving Key Task 3 (meet company statutory and legal obligations) is €263K. The question should then be asked as to whether

TABLE 5.1 Finance department budget for 2013

Resource	2012 €000s	2013 €000s	Key task Reference	Comments
Salaries	210	218	3	Inflationary pay increase 4 per cent
National insurance	11	12	3	Budget increase
Training	20	5	2	Reduction due to staff retention
Stationery	5	3	3	New supplier
Travel	20	5	4	Branch closure requires fewer trips
Recruitment costs	30	5	3	Expected staff retention
Entertainment	2	0	3	Not required
Accounting software	0	8	3	New software required at current prices
Share of overheads	16	17	3	Inflation increase 4 per cent
Total	**314**	**273**		

this task could be outsourced to a professional firm at a lower cost. The costs of all key tasks should be calculated and compared with typical outsourced costs.

Some departments will require additional capital equipment. This is prepared on a different form from operating expenditure. A capital budget relates to the purchase of new fixed assets. Capital costs for fixed assets are not consumed within the budget year but may span many years. For example, a car might be used in the business for five years. Typical items of capital expenditure are: plant and equipment, vehicles, furniture and fittings, buildings, improvement (not repairs) to existing assets and large main-frame-type computer installations. Smaller computers are often assumed to be written off in the year of purchase and are treated as operating expenditure rather then capital.

Capital budgets will have to be justified in that they must support the overall organizational goals. It may be that new plant is required for a new opportunity that has been identified in the plan or that there is an opportunity to improve efficiency. The planning process should recognize an opportunity, which will then be considered by the appropriate operating department. It will then be evaluated and a decision made as to whether to proceed or not. Capital expenditure will also have specific funding implications and additional long-term funds will need to be found.

Capital budget process:

- recognition of an opportunity;
- link with overall corporate goals;
- initial costings;
- identification of financial benefits;
- evaluation, net present value, payback etc;
- identification of alternatives;
- proposal;
- decision.

Once the decision has been made to undertake the capital project the department responsible should submit details to the finance department as follows:

2013 Capital expenditure budget Production Department

Description of asset	Expected life in years	Cost (€000s)	Month
Cutting machine	5	50	July
Delivery van	6	30	August

From the above return the accountant will be able to arrange suitable long-term funds and also calculate the amount of depreciation to charge into the operating expenditure budget. S/he will also ensure that appropriate taxation allowances are claimed for the annual allowable element of the capital expenditure. In some countries these are called capital allowances. We will explore capital budgets in some detail later in this chapter.

Reporting of actual expenditure against budget

Table 5.2 is an example of a year-to-date budget v actual expenditure report in €000s.

TABLE 5.2 Example of a year-to-date budget v actual expenditure report in €000s

Resources	YTD Budget	YTD Actual	Total Variance	Additional Rate	Outlay	Timing
Salaries	250	240	10		10	
Travel	30	35	(5)	(5)		
Entertainment	10	5	5		5	
Stationery	20	25	(5)	(5)		
Training	30	40	(10)	(5)	(5)	
Allocated overheads	70	70	0			
Totals	410	415	(5)	(10)	0	5

NOTES:

1 Year-to-date (YTD) figures are shown only. This is generally the most informative level at which to report. A separate report can be prepared to show current month values can also be prepared if required.

2 A report similar to this will be prepared for each department.

3 The total variance is reported with adverse variances shown in brackets.

4 The analysis of the total variance can be explained in three columns, rate, additional outlay and timing. These should be completed by the budget holder.

5 Rate = a change in the rate (price) from that anticipated in the budget. For example, the budget may have assumed a 3% increase in training fees when in fact they increased by 10%.

6 Additional outlay = purchasing more (or less if favourable) of a resource but at the same price.

7 Timing = the expenditure is earlier or later than expected.

Example:

Budget is for 10 rolls of paper @ €5 per roll	€50
Actual is 12 rolls of paper @ €4 per roll	€48
Total Variance is	€2 Favourable
Due to:	
Additional Outlay – 2 rolls @ €5	€10 Adverse
Rate – 12 rolls @ (€4–€5)	€12 Favourable
Total Variance is	€2 Favourable

Most variances can be explained in the above categories of rate, additional outlay and timing. It is helpful if budget holders can use this discipline so that a consolidated variance analysis can be prepared. Budget holders will normally provide comments for the variances in addition to the analysis classifications.

Some key departmental budgets

Most organizations will require the managers of each department (the budget holders) to produce a budget. Budget holders should be responsible for the expenditure that they can control. Once their budget has been approved they will be responsible for controlling expenditure against their budget and this will be done at the point of commitment, assisted by periodic reporting of actual against budgeted expenditure.

Key budgets in most organizations are:

- sales revenue budget;
- production budget;
- materials budget;
- labour budget;
- overhead budgets;
- capital budget;
- sales budget.

The sales budget is one of the key budgets in an organization because most other departmental budgets depend upon and support its requirements. For example, the production and transportation budget will depend on how much product is to be sold and delivered.

The sales budget will show volumes and prices for each product to be sold. The volume forecast to be sold will depend upon demand

and the ability to compete and fulfil, and the price will depend upon competitive factors, supply and demand.

When preparing a sales budget the sales director will take account of the following factors:

- the value of organizational growth required;
- the ability of the organization to manufacture and deliver;
- production capacity ceilings;
- demand for products and services;
- pricing;
- market trends and future direction;
- competition both existing and potential;
- organizational limiting factors;
- channels to market;
- distribution and operational strategies;
- marketing strategies;
- sales force ability and resources;
- advertising budget.

The price of a product is set by the market. In an efficient market it will be set by the interaction of supply and demand. Supply will be affected by competitors offering the same or alternative products. Demand will be affected by the need for and ability to purchase a product in a market. The sales director will work closely with the marketing director to determine both price and volume budgets. Setting a sales budget requires an in-depth understanding of the market and competition.

An example of a sales budget for a company selling rigid inflatable boats is given in Table 5.3.

TABLE 5.3   Sales budget 2013

Product/ model	Forecast volumes	Unit price (€)	Sales revenue (€)
3 metre	500	800	400,000
4 metre	300	1,000	300,000
5 metre	100	2,000	200,000
6 metre	50	5,000	250,000
Total			1,150,000

Before a sales budget is finally agreed a reality check is essential, since there is no room for reckless optimism. This is because so many other things 'hang off' the sales budget. Production capacity, sales force recruitment, advertising budgets and capital budgets are just a few of the commitments that might depend on sales budget accuracy. A company could get into serious difficulty by getting the sales budget wrong. For example, one sales manager was optimistic that sales indications from an overseas agent were realistic! They were but they would end up in an existing fulfilled territory, resulting in no additional sales.

A few final reality checks might include:

- What is the basis for the volume assumptions?
- Is there production capacity to meet the forecast sales volumes?
- Do forecast sales fit with the company's overall plans?
- Is the demand real?
- Are growth figures real?
- Are territory/volume assumptions correct?
- Have we correctly analysed the competition?
- Are prices realistic?
- Can the marketing department really provide the promotion required?
- How accurate has the sales director been in the past with sales forecasts?

When the sales budget has been agreed a company can proceed to prepare a production budget.

Production volume budget

The production volume budget will determine the production hours required to produce the volumes of products required in the sales budget taking into account any opening and closing stocks. An example is shown in Table 5.4.

To meet the sales budget and the required stock level will require the building of 980 units. We now calculate production hours and also consider what effect this will have on plant capacity. To do this we will prepare a plant utilization budget (Table 5.5). As the table shows, we have identified a limiting factor. The assembly plant has a capacity shortage of 120 hours. A decision will now be made. Either increase plant capacity (which will have an effect on the capital budget and on

TABLE 5.4 Production budget

Product/ model	Forecast volumes	Opening stock	Closing stock	Production required
3 metre	500	0	10	510
4 metre	300	20	20	300
5 metre	100	5	15	110
6 metre	50	2	12	60
Total production required				980

TABLE 5.5 Plant utilization budget – assembly department

Product model	Production volume	Assembly unit hours	Assembly hours
3 metre	510	8	4,080
4 metre	300	10	3,000
5 metre	110	12	1,320
6 metre	60	12	720
Total assembly hours			9,120
Assembly plant capacity			9,000
Capacity shortage			(120)

the cash budget) or simply do not fulfil the sale budget volumes. This is an example of the iterative process that is part of budgeting, and also an example of how the sales budget affects other budgets.

There will, of course, be many stages in the production of this product. We have just considered the assembly department. Other departments might include mouldings, painting and testing, each of which will have its own limiting factors.

Now that we have worked out the number of hours required in the assembly department we can prepare a direct labour budget and a direct materials budget.

Direct labour budget

The direct labour budget takes the required labour hours from the production budget and calculates the cost of labour using standard and overtime labour rates and the number of employees required.

Direct labour budget for assembly 2013

The assembly process requires 9,120 assembly hours and this can be performed by five men working 40 hours per week plus a little overtime.

Assuming labour rates are €12 per hour for normal time, €18 per hour for overtime and that a standard working week is 40 hours over 45 weeks per year, the labour cost will be:

Standard hours (5 × 40 × 45) = 9,000 hours @ €12 = €108,000

Overtime hours = 120 hours @ €18   = €2,160

Totals = 9,120 hours   = €110,160

The direct labour budget for the assembly plant will, therefore, be:

Labour cost   €110,160
Employee numbers   5

A labour budget will be prepared for each production process and, if a standard costing system is used, the labour rates will become the standard rates used. Standard costing systems will be discussed in the chapter on costing.

Any expenditure variances against the labour budget will generally be due either to rate, additional hours or slippage.

The direct materials budget

The direct materials budget will determine how much material or what components are required to produce the production budget volumes. For the assembly process it could look like Table 5.6.

TABLE 5.6 Direct materials budget

Component	Qty 3m	Qty 4m	Qty 5m	Qty 6m	Total Qty	Unit cost (€)	Total cost (€)
Tubes (metres)	3,060	2,400	1,100	720	7,280	5	36,400
Soles	510	300	110	60	980	40	39,200
Thwarts	510	300	110	60	980	7	6,860
Rope (metres)	4,590	3,600	1,650	1,080	10,920	1.5	16,380
Hulls (metres)	1,530	1,200	550	360	3,640	30	109,200
Glue (litres)	510	400	185	120	1,215	30	36,450
Eyes	510	300	110	60	980	5	4,900
Oars	1,020	600	220	120	1,960	40	74,800
Oar crutches	1,020	600	220	120	1,960	10	19,600
Total							343,790

The total material cost of assembling the production budget requirement is €343,790. The unit costs shown above will form the standard
material costs for the period.

Budgeted contribution

We have now completed the sales budget and the direct labour and
material budgets for assembly.

Assuming that there was only one other manufacturing process
and that the direct labour budget for this was €30,000 and the direct

materials budget (paint) was €10,000, then the budgeted contribution (gross profit percentage) would be:

Sales	1,150,000
Direct labour 110,160 + 30,000	(140,160)
Direct materials 343,790 + 10,000	(353,790)
Gross profit	656,050
Gross margin per cent = 656,050/1,150,000	**57 per cent**

This is the gross profit before overheads. It shows the contribution a sale makes after deducting the direct costs towards fixed overhead expenses and profits. Note that most of the direct costs are considered to be variable in that they vary with a level of production. Less production should mean fewer costs.

The gross margin percentage is one of the key 'dash board' figures in a company and will be carefully monitored each time a sale is made.

Overhead expenditure budgets

Many departments in a company are not directly involved in the manufacturing or production process but support it in some way. These may include the human resources, finance and stock control departments. The costs of running these departments tend not to vary with the level of production in the way that direct costs do. Within a budget period they are either fixed or semi-fixed.

These budgets must be prepared on a zero basis by estimating the resources required to deliver the departmental objectives. The cost of these departments may also be compared with the cost of using an outsourced service or a shared service. The previous year's expenditure is usually shown on the budget work sheet as a guide to costs but this should not be used as a fundamental base for the current budget. An example of a typical departmental overhead budget is given in Table 5.7.

This Finance Department budget supports the following key tasks identified in the plan:

- meet statutory obligations to maintain proper accounts and file annual return;
- maintain VAT and other taxation records;
- pay staff, run payroll, keep NI and PAYE records;
- maintain supplier accounts and ensure payments;

TABLE 5.7 Finance department budget for 2013 (€000s)

Expenditure type	2012 budget	2012 actual	2013 budget	Comments
Salaries	50	51	53	4% increase
Bonuses	5	4	5	10% for on target
Travel	10	1	8	Audit branches
Training	3	2	3	CPE courses
Vehicle exp.	7	6	7	Lease plus running costs
Entertainment	2	1	0	Nothing planned
Office space	7	6	6	Rent, rates, light, heat apportioned
Stationery	4	3	3	Quoted from supplier
Software	2	2	0	No new software planned
IT support	5	4	5	Contracted rate for IT support
Telephone	1	1	1	Annual usage
Temp staff	3	5	3	For possible illness
Totals	**99**	**86**	**94**	

- maintain debtors ledger and credit control;
- prepare product costings;
- prepare internal budgets and management accounts;
- maintain cash records and bank accounts;
- obtain audit clearance;
- provide strategic financial advice to the board.

It may be possible to allocate the €94K resource budget across the above 10 tasks in order to compare them with outside costs and outsourced services.

For example, of the €94K budget it might be estimated on a time-apportioned basis that the costs attributable to the payroll task are €15K. If it is possible to get payroll outsourced at a cost of only €10K then it might be worthwhile considering this. However, as is often the case, by outsourcing payroll the company might not lose the whole of the €15K of internal costs apportioned because staff perform more than one function and cannot be easily separated. However, there might be a case for outsourcing and in any case this type of exercise does highlight inefficiencies. Of course, outsourcing is more than a financial decision. Quality, continuity and a whole lot more factors come into the equation.

The finance department costs tend to be fixed or semi-fixed during the budget period. Staff can be laid off but notice periods and redundancy pay may offset or partially offset any savings in the year. However, some other departments may have costs of a more variable nature. For example the sales department's salaries and bonuses may vary with sales levels because sales staff are often paid commissions.

The costs of a department are sometimes allocated to an identified internal customer (another cost centre). The reasoning behind this is that it shows the full costs incurred by a particular department. For example, the finance department might allocate payroll management costs to all other departments on the basis of personnel numbers. The method for doing this is internal charging. Some finance directors do not like internal charging because it can become confusing and there is an argument that there is little point in allocating a cost out to managers if they cannot directly control that cost. I mention it here because most companies have some limited form of cost allocation to departments.

Research and development budget

Research costs may be considered under two major classifications:

- pure research, where there is no specific product yet developed;
- applied research, where the work related to the development of a specific product offering.

For the sake of this explanation a product is something that a customer recognizes and might buy.

TABLE 5.8   Research and development budget for 2013 (€000s)

Resource	Total budget	Pure Project 1	Pure Project 2	Applied Project 1
Salaries	90,000	40,000	40,000	10,000
Materials	20,000	10,000	5,000	5,000
Licenses	2,000	0	0	2,000
Lab costs	6,000	2,000	2,000	2,000
Totals	**118,000**	**52,000**	**47,000**	**19,000**

The accounting and taxation treatments of pure and applied research are different and they need to be accounted for separately.

A research and development budget should show the costs of each project and differentiate between pure and applied research cost as in Table 5.8.

Capital budgets

I briefly mentioned capital budgeting earlier in this chapter. We will now explain how the whole capital budgeting process works.

To start I will define capital expenditure, which is sometimes called CAPEX:

Capital expenditure relates to items that are not consumed by the business within the budget period but are used over a number of years. They are items of a permanent nature. Examples of capital expenditure are:

- buildings;
- plant and equipment;
- vehicles;
- improvement to existing assets (but not replacements);
- furniture and fittings of a permanent nature;
- large main frame type computers (generally not PCs).

Expenditure such as software, stationery and materials is not permanent but is consumed within the year and is called revenue expenditure.

This sort of expenditure is written off to the profit-and-loss account each year.

Capital expenditure is not totally consumed within the budget year and is not written off to the profit-and-loss account. Instead it is shown in the balance sheet as an asset. A portion of capital expenditure may be used within the year and this is the amount by which an asset depreciates. Depreciation is usually calculated by dividing the asset cost by the expected life. The resultant figure will be the figure used for depreciation. This can be done on a straight-line basis or a reducing-balance basis depending on the expected depreciation profile of the asset. For example, an asset costing €10,000 that will last five years with a nil residual value would be depreciated at €2,000 p.a. using the straight-line basis. There are other methods of calculating depreciation, such as the mileage of a vehicle. The point here is that the amount of depreciation calculated is written off to the profit-and-loss account and the value of the asset in the balance sheet will be reduced by the same amount.

As previously mentioned, the taxation treatment for capital expenditure is usually through a system of capital allowances. Therefore, to calculate the taxable profit it is normal to add back accounting depreciation and deduct capital allowance from the accounting profit.

In addition to requiring different accounting treatment, capital expenditure requires special approval and sanctioning because it is an investment decision rather than an ongoing operational decision as is the case with operating/revenue expenditure.

Different companies have different processes for capital investment decisions. Probably one of the best methods was that identified by Paul King of Queens College, Cambridge. He wrote several papers explaining the decision process where he identified the stages involved in capital investment decisions. These included 'Capital investment decisions' (1967) and 'Is the emphasis on capital budgeting theory misplaced?' (1974). I have not identified any better method so will use his stages below.

The principal stages in capital investment decisions as identified by Paul King are shown in Figure 5.3. Once a capital budget has been approved by the board, the executive responsible for developing the project will normally be required to go back for capital expenditure approval before a final order is placed. Before making a commitment it will be necessary to arrange suitable long-term funds. Capital projects require long-term funds, either loan or equity capital. A capital budget is shown in Table 5.9.

FIGURE 5.3 Principal stages in capital investment decisions

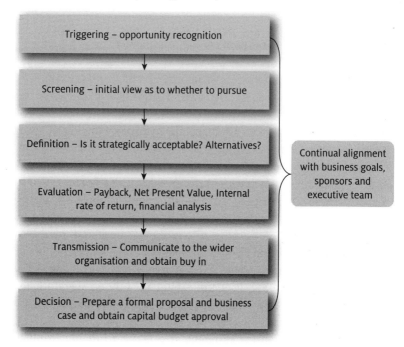

TABLE 5.9 Capital budget for 2013 (€000s)

Project	Q1	Q2	Q3	Q4	Total
Extension to paint shop		30			30
Additional plant capacity	10	10	10	10	40
HGV			140		140
Warehouse in Essex		240			240
Totals	**10**	**280**	**150**	**10**	**450**
Funding:					
5-year term loan for paint shop and plant	70				
Vehicle lease for HGV	140				
15-year mortgage for warehouse	240				
	450				

Capital rationing

Because capital is often scarce it is not always possible to undertake all of the capital projects in a budget. Choices will have to be made and, all other things being equal, the choices made will seek to maximize overall profits. Projects can be ranked in terms of their net present value (NPV). The NPV is simply the total of the present values of the cash flow of a project.

The present value (PV) of a future value (FV) is simply:

$$PV = \frac{FV \times 1}{(1+r)^n}$$

Where:
PV = Present value
FV = Future value
r = Compound rate of interest or discount rate
n = the period or number of years

For example, if a project would yield €5,000 in three years' time when the rate of inflation was 5 per cent the present value would be:

$$PV = \frac{€5,000 \times 1}{(1+0.05)^3}$$

$$PV = \frac{€5,000 \times 1}{1.158}$$

$$PV = €5,000 \times 0.864$$

$$PV = €4,318$$

If we have a number of projects that we can invest in but only a limited amount of capital to invest, then we will seek to maximize our return by investing in those that produce the highest net present value.

For example, suppose we have €1,900 to invest and there are three project options that produce different returns as follows:

Project	Outlay (€)	NPV (€)	Return
Project 1	500	250	50 per cent
Project 2	900	405	45 per cent
Project 3	700	266	38 per cent
Totals	**2,100**	**921**	**44 per cent**

If we assume that the projects have to be completed either in total or not at all, we might wish to select Project 2 and Project 3 since this would produce the highest net present value:

Project	Outlay (€)	NPV (€)	Return
Project 2	900	405	45 per cent
Project 3	700	266	38 per cent
Total	**1,600**	**671**	**42 per cent**

By choosing to invest €1,600 of our €1,900 in Projects 2 and 3 we would achieve a net present value of €671.

If we chose Projects 1 and 2 our net present value would only be €655 (250 + 405). However, we would only have invested €1,400 (500 + 900) and our return as a percentage would be greater at 47 per cent (655/1400).

So we have choices:

● Invest €1,600 in projects 2 and 3 and get a return of 42 per cent to produce a net present value of €671;

or

● Invest €1,400 in projects 1 and 2 and get a return of 47 per cent to produce a net present value of €655.

Assuming that there were no other investment opportunities and that the projects were not 'divisible', the company might seek to maximize the net present value even though this produces a lower return on its investment. However, it might decide to invest fewer funds at a greater return percentage, thereby keeping its funds intact for potential future opportunities.

Capital rationing decisions can get complicated in large companies with multiple options, and the above simple example will give you an idea of the considerations and methods that might be adopted. However, there are often many other factors that need to be taken into account, such as the probability of project returns that might need to be factored in.

When an organization finds that it is rejecting profitable projects because of limited capital it will, of course, seek to remove those capital constraints. There are many ways of doing this, such as finding a joint venture partner, selling and leasing back property, improving debt collection, using invoice finance and many more. Some of these options may reduce the return on a project.

Summary

In this chapter we have discussed how budgets are initiated and support the planning process and how the budget cycle works. We have explained the major types of departmental budget and how they are monitored and controlled, together with variance analysis. An explanation of the differences between operating expenditure budgets and capital budgets has been provided as well as the elements of capital rationing.

You should now understand:

- the integration of budgets with plans;
- types of departmental operating budgets;
- variance analysis techniques;
- capital budgeting;
- capital rationing issues and solutions.

Budgeting provides an important control tool for strategic financial management. Case 10 in Chapter 16 (page 223) demonstrates some of the practical benefits of integrating the budgeting and planning process.

CHAPTER SIX

PRODUCT AND SERVICE COSTING AND PRICING

In this chapter we will discuss some of the principal methods of costing products and services, and how these may be used to determine profitability. Selling prices are, of course, determined by the market but an understanding of costs is essential in order to ensure that profitable sales are pursued.

We will discuss:

- types of cost;
- contribution, break-even point and marginal costing;
- absorption costing/standard costing;
- selling prices and the sales mix.

Types of cost: fixed, variable, semi-variable

Three classifications of cost are:

- fixed costs;
- variable costs;
- semi-variable costs.

Cost may also be called 'direct' – where they can be directly attributed to a particular product or service – or 'indirect' when they do not directly relate to a product or service. The three classifications are explained below.

Fixed costs

Fixed costs are those that do not change within the budget period, which is usually one year. They are fixed at the start of the year and do not change substantially or at all with levels of production or other variable factors. Examples of fixed costs are:

- management salaries (excluding performance bonuses);
- rent;
- business rates;
- insurance premiums;
- taxes;
- depreciation (but see semi-variable costs below).

It is unlikely that once agreed these types of cost will change within the year. For example, rent is usually fixed at the start of the period and so are rates and insurance. It can be argued that, over time, all costs can change. However, for our purposes we can assume that the above types of cost will remain largely fixed during the year.

Variable costs

Variable costs are the types of cost that will change given different levels of production, output or sales. For example, the total cost of vehicle fuel used in a year will depend on the miles driven by the vehicle. Fuel, would, therefore, be considered a variable cost. Common examples of variables costs are:

- direct materials;
- direct labour;
- machine power.

Any costs that vary with different levels of activity are variable costs.

Semi-variable costs

There is a type of cost that is difficult to classify as either fixed or variable. This type of cost can be called semi-variable. An example could be storage rent, which goes up when an existing storage facility is full and another one is hired. Depreciation, which we have classified as a fixed cost above, may in fact be semi-variable because an item of capital equipment may depreciate more if it is used more. Depreciation may vary according to activity but it may also be related (and fixed) to a period of time. It could both vary and be fixed and, therefore, a semi-variable cost. Some costs are fixed to a certain level of activity and then increase once that level is exceeded. This type of cost would be semi-variable.

Total cost and unit costs

The total cost is simply the total of all costs at a given level of activity. The unit cost is the cost attributed to a single production unit.

Given that total cost includes variable costs, we can expect it to increase with activity levels. Unit costs should decrease when activity increases because, within certain limits, fixed costs do not change and will be absorbed over a greater volume of units produced.

These concepts are best explained by means of examples:

Examples

A company that manufactures filters has fixed costs (rent and rates) of €150,000 per year. The variable costs (direct materials and labour) are €5 per unit and it produces 60,000 units per year

Fixed costs	€150,000
Variable costs (60,000 × 5)	€300,000
Total cost	€450,000
Unit cost of one filter (450,000/60,000)	€7.50

If production is increased to 70,000 units (filters) per year we will see that, although total costs increase, the unit cost of one filter decreases.

Fixed cost	€150,000
Variable costs (70,000 × 5)	€350,000
Total cost	€500,000
Unit cost of one filter (500,000/70,000)	€7.14

So, if we increase production we can expect a greater profit margin when a unit is sold. This will remain true until we reach a capacity ceiling and have to invest in greater capacity, thereby increasing the level of fixed costs. You can see, therefore, that once a capacity ceiling has been reached a substantial increase in production will be needed in order to avoid increasing unit costs.

For example, if the capacity of the factory was 72,000 units and to accommodate an increase in production to 144,000 units would require additional fixed costs of €100,000, then it might not be worthwhile making the investment if sales of the units could only be increased to 80,000.

New fixed costs (150,000 + 100,000)	€250,000
Variable costs (80,000 × 5)	€400,000
Total cost	€650,000
Unit cost of one filter (650,000/80,000)	€8.13

The rise in fixed costs has resulted in an increase in unit cost to €8.13 per filter produced/sold. It might not, therefore, be profitable to make this investment unless increased levels of sales/production could be guaranteed.

Contribution, break-even point and marginal costing

Understanding contribution and the break-even point is one of the most important aspects of costing and price/volume decision making. It is a simple concept and is best explained by means of an example.

Contribution

Contribution is sometime referred to as gross margin or gross profit. It is the contribution that sales value after the deduction of variable costs makes towards fixed overheads and profits.

For example if a product sells for €10 per unit and its variable cost per unit is €4 then it makes a contribution of €6 per unit. Contribution may also be expressed as a percentage of sales. In this case it would be 60 per cent (6/10).

If sales were 100,000 units and fixed costs were €400,000 per year the contribution and profit would be:

	Volume	Unit €	Total €
Sales	100,000	10	1,000,000
Variable cost	100,000	4	400,000
Contribution		6	600,000
Fixed costs			400,000
Net profit			200,000

Break-even point

This is the point at which the contribution just covers fixed costs. At a certain level of activity the volume sold/produced multiplied by the unit contribution will cover the fixed costs. For example, in the above case if we sold 66,667 units we would achieve a contribution of €400,000 and this is exactly equal to the level of fixed costs.

$$\text{Break-even volume} = \frac{\text{Fixed costs}}{\text{Unit contribution}}$$

$$\text{Break-even volume} = \frac{400,000}{6}$$

$$\text{Break-even volume} = 66,667 \text{ units}$$

If we sell more than 66,667 units we will make a net profit, if we sell exactly 66,667 units we will cover all of our fixed costs, and if we sell fewer than 66,667 units we will not even cover our fixed costs and we will make a net loss.

Given certain levels of expected sales, break-even analysis can also be used to determine if a selling price will produce a net profit, a net loss or just cover fixed costs.

Example:

A company expects to sell 100,000 units. Variable costs are €6 per unit. Fixed costs are €400,000 per year At what price would the company break-even?

Solution:
To break even the company needs to cover €400,000 of fixed costs. It will need a contribution of €400,000 from the 100,000 units sold. This

is a unit contribution of €4 (€400,000/100,000). Now, since the variable cost is €6 per unit the selling price to break even will be €10 per unit (€4 + €6).

$$\text{Break-even selling price} = \frac{\text{Fixed costs}}{\text{Volume}} + \text{Variable unit cost}$$

$$\text{Break-even selling price} = \frac{400,000}{100,000} + 6$$

Break-even selling price = 4 + 6
Break-even selling price = **10**

Proof:

100,000 units @ €10 selling price = €1,000,000
100,000 units @ €6 variable cost = €600,000
Contribution = €400,000
Fixed costs = €400,000
Net profit = Nil

Knowing the break-even selling price is extremely useful. For example:

● If we sell at €10 we know we will cover all costs.
● If we sell at €11 we know we will cover all costs and make a net profit.
● If we sell at €9 we know that we will not cover all costs and make a net loss.

Therefore, if the competition is selling at €10 and we cannot charge more than this, then we must decide whether to sell for €10 and at least cover our fixed costs. Fixed costs will not go away in the budget period and it might be better to at least cover them. Any selling price that covers variable costs will make a contribution towards fixed costs, and when considering product prices there may be an argument to accept a price that will at least make a contribution. However, a company cannot survive on overall net losses.

Another example of a break-even point is illustrated in Figure 6.1 below:

FIGURE 6.1 The break-even point

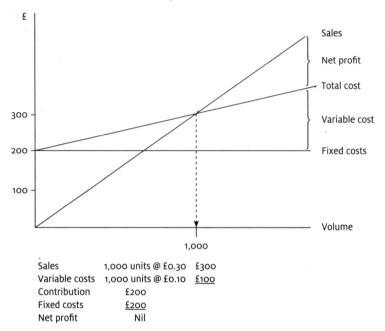

Sales	1,000 units @ £0.30	£300
Variable costs	1,000 units @ £0.10	£100
Contribution	£200	
Fixed costs	£200	
Net profit	Nil	

This graph illustrates the break-even point. At a volume of 1,000 units the total cost line and the sales line intersect at the value £300, where total costs equal total sales revenue.

Using break-even analysis for strategic decisions

Break-even analysis can be a particularly useful aid to making strategic decisions. It is simple to use and can provide a quick assessment of different strategic options, as is illustrated in the following example.

Example

A manufacturing company is considering launching a new product into a market that already has a number of existing suppliers. The total market value to all suppliers is about €6.5 million, which represents 500,000 units.

The company wants to evaluate two strategies. Strategy 1 is a higher-priced higher-quality product and Strategy 2 is a lower-priced product.

The higher-priced product will produce a higher unit margin but lower volumes, and the lower-priced product will produce a smaller margin but should produce a higher volume.

	Strategy 1	**Strategy 2**
Unit selling price	€15	€13
Unit variable cost	€8	€5
Unit contribution	€7 (47 per cent)	€8 (62 per cent)
Fixed costs per year	€600,000	€600,000
Number of units required to be sold to break even*	85,714	75,000
Total market size	500,000	500,000
Percentage of market required to break even	17.1 per cent	15 per cent

* fixed costs/unit contribution

Strategy 2 requires a smaller level of market penetration to break even. This can now be considered against market research data that indicates the feasibility of a lower-priced lower-quality product being accepted in the market.

The use of the break-even point and contribution analysis are the fundamental components of marginal costing, which costs products on a marginal basis rather than a fully cost absorbed basis. The advantages and disadvantages of marginal costing are discussed below.

Advantages

- Marginal costing is most useful to show the relative contribution each product makes. It is useful for comparisons.
- It is simple to understand and shows a very clear picture of the relationship between cost, selling prices and volumes.
- It is used as one of a company's 'dashboard indicators' to show key performance indicators at a glance.
- It can be used in sales-mix-type decisions to maximize contribution and profits.
- There is no arbitrary allocation or spreading of fixed overheads to products.
- The separation of fixed and variable costs enables clearer understanding and better business decisions.

Disadvantages

- Marginal costing does not show the full cost of a product.
- Marginal costing may be misunderstood and sales decisions may be made without an understanding of a full product cost.
- It is possible to use a mixture of both marginal and fully absorbed costing.

Absorption costing – standard costing

Absorption costing, as its name implies, fully absorbs all costs (both fixed and variable) into product costs. It gives an understanding of the total cost of a product based upon certain assumptions regarding how costs are allocated. It can get complicated but does have certain advantages if the system is operated correctly and understood. Unfortunately, this is often not the case and many companies have made poor business decisions based upon poor absorption costing systems. A major absorption costing system is standard costing. This type of system can be fully integrated into the financial accounts and it is the system that we will explain below. Most manufacturing companies use standard costing, sometimes in conjunction with marginal costing.

The fully integrated standard costing system

This system sets standards for costs and these costs are absorbed into product costs. Variances from standards are measured and management actions are taken as a result of understanding variances. It is a form of management by exception.

The cost of a product is explained in terms of materials, labour and overheads and standards are set for these as follows:

Materials	Standard prices	Standard quantities
Labour	Standard rates	Standard times
Overheads	Standard absorption rate (see below)	

The standard absorption rate is based upon the capacity of an overhead facility and the time taken to produce a unit in that facility.

Standards are set annually (or more often) and the costs of products are calculated using these standard costs. The amount of material used, the labour hours and the time taken by the product in the factory will be used in conjunction with the standard rates to calculate unit product costs.

Of course, actual prices, quantities used, labour rates and times taken will be different from the standard rates and variances will be measured. The variances measured under a standard costing system are:

- *Material price variance* – This is the difference between actual prices and standard prices measured over the actual quantity used.
- *Material usage variance* – This is the difference between the actual amount of material used and the standard amount allowed all at the standard price.
- *Labour rate variance* – The difference between actual rates paid and standard labour rates over the actual hours worked.
- *Labour efficiency variance* – The difference between the actual time taken and the standard time allowed at the standard rate of pay.
- *Overhead budget expenditure variance* – A measure of buying efficiency that is the difference between the actual and budgeted overheads.
- *Overhead efficiency variance* – This is the standard time less the actual time at the standard overhead rate. It shows the effect of labour efficiency on overhead absorption.
- *Overhead volume variance* – This is the actual level of activity less the standard level of activity at the standard rate. It shows whether plant is being utilized.

The standard costing system is integrated into the financial accounting system. An example of accounting entries is given below:

Example:

A company sets a standard of 20p for a material price.
It purchases 1,000 units at 21p each.
The material price variance will be: 1,000 (21p-20p) or €10 adverse
The standard cost was 1,000 @ 20p:€200
The actual cost was 1,000 @ 21p:€210
The total variance was: €10 adverse
Due to:
Material price: €10 adverse

Using the fully integrated standard costing system the entries in the accounts in respect to the purchase of materials will be:

Debit materials account: €200 (with actual quantity purchased @ standard rate)

Debit material price variance account: €10 (with actual price less standard price × actual quantity)

Credit supplier account: €210 (with the goods value on the invoice, 1,000 @ 21p)

As goods pass through the production process into work in progress and eventually into finished stocks, entries are made in the accounts at standard rates and allowances. There is no need for you to work through all of these laborious entries since this is a management text and an understanding of reports and accounts presented to you is all that is required. However, the accounting entries are shown in Figure 6.2 below:

Using the diagram you can trace the accounting entries. For example the raw materials account is debited with the actual quantity of goods purchased at the standard rate, and the variance between actual and standard prices using the actual volume is debited or credited to the material price variance. Materials used in production are debited to the work in progress account, and the variance between the standard allowance and the actual allowance is debited or credited to the material usage variance account. Labour and overheads are absorbed into work in progress, variances measured and as products are completed they are transferred into the finished stock account at standard rates.

Two of the great benefits of the fully integrated standard costing system are:

● Integrity of information: it is integrated fully with main financial accounting systems.
● A dashboard approach that gives management a quick view on areas that need attention.

The type of information produced by a standard costing system and actions that can be taken by management are listed in Table 6.1.

FIGURE 6.2 The fully integrated standard costing system process

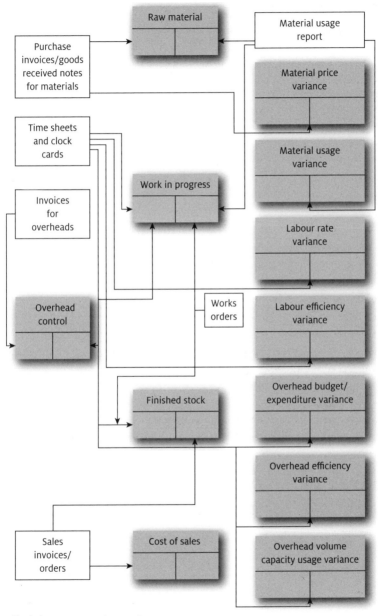

Shaded areas represent accounts.

TABLE 6.1 Information produced by a standard costing system and relevant actions

Variance	Possible reasons	Possible actions
Material price	Changes in price Inflation assumptions wrong	Compare alternative suppliers Review budget estimates
Material usage	Using more or less in production	Look for wastage, check controls, review estimates and budgets
Labour rate	Paying staff more or less Staff mix different from standard	Revise costings and budgets If adverse see if a more favourable mix can be achieved Review budgets
Labour efficiency	Times taken to complete a job different from standard	Measure job times Review budgets and costs
Overhead expenditure	Actuals different from standard	Review suppliers Review budgets/costs
Overhead capacity use	Usage standards incorrect	Measure and review capacity
O'hd volume efficiency	Times taken different from standard	Measure job time Review budgets

The theory is that if standards and assumptions set during the budget process achieve an acceptable result then, by constantly measuring variances from standards and taking remedial actions, management stand a better chance of achieving their goals.

However, just a quick glance at this process will demonstrate how it can get complicated and can confuse. Clearly, in a large manufacturing company (a car manufacturer for example) a standard costing system has great value. However, many smaller companies use the system without the resources to ensure accuracy and without a management team that fully appreciates how the system works. For this reason I would suggest that it is more suitable for larger companies. As a manager you may come across this system and I hope that the above has explained the essential process and benefits.

Case study 8 in Chapter 16 (page 000) compares the use and mis-use of marginal with full absorption costing (standard costing) information in pricing decisions.

Activity-based costing (ABC)

Activity-based costing assigns costs to activities and then to products. It is, therefore, another technique for allocating indirect costs to products.

A traditional costing method usually assigns overhead costs to products on the basis of an average absorption rate. ABC first of all assigns indirect costs to activities and then assigns the costs to products on the basis of the products' usage of the activities. It attempts to identify cause-and-effect relationships in order to accurately allocate costs to products. ABC is useful when indirect cost allocation accuracy is important and when indirect costs are a large proportion of total costs. It is commonly used in the manufacturing sector.

The four steps in the activity-based costing process are:

1 Recognize and list the activities in the value chain related to the production process of the product.

2 Estimate a total cost for each of the activities listed above.

3 Compute a cost-driver rate for each activity on the basis of an allocation method that has a direct link to the cost of the activity. See example below.

4 Apply these activity costs to products using the cost-driver rate.

Example

A company classifies paint-room maintenance as an indirect cost activity for the metal lamp shades it manufactures. The company estimates paint-room maintenance costs to be €3,000 per month and determines that batches of lamp shades sprayed in the paint room are an appropriate cost-driver allocation base for paint-room costs. The paint room produces 750 batches per month. Thus, the cost-driver rate would be €3,000/750, or €3.00 per batch. Therefore, the company would apply €3.00 of indirect cost for each batch produced by the paint room.

Activity-based costing is often used as an aid to strategic decisions concerning processes, outsourcing and selling prices.

Selling prices and the sales mix

This chapter has been concerned with costing methods that will help you understand the profitability of products sold. These methods will indicate whether pricing decisions are acceptable and produce the desired return.

Selling prices are not set from costs. They are set by the market. A sales price, in an efficient market, is set by the interaction of supply and demand. When setting a selling price the sales director will want to set one that will enable volume targets to be met. S/he will do this with an expert knowledge of the market, customers' needs and the competition. The director will also need to know what the lowest price is that is acceptable and in particular will need to know product contributions in order to determine sales mixes.

When setting a selling price an organization may have a wide variety of motives; however, pricing does have both social and legal consequences that need to be taken into account. For example, price fixing is illegal in most countries. Deceptive prices may fall foul of increasing legislation, and predatory pricing is not allowed in many countries. Price discrimination is also illegal in many countries. With this in mind it is wise that price setting does at least not offend these basic rules.

A company will normally want to set an optimal price that will maximize its profitability. However, there may be other reasons. For example revenue maximization and cash flow may be more important than profit. Sales growth and market penetration may be a priority. Selling prices will depend to an extent on sales and marketing strategy.

The sales mix

Using marginal costing/contribution information can be very useful in determining the optimal mix of products to be sold.

It is possible that, although overall sales values and volumes are on target, a hidden adverse sales mix is reducing profitability. The example in Table 6.2 illustrates how analysing a sales mix variance using gross margin percentages can expose the effect an adverse sales mix has on profits.

TABLE 6.2 Analysis of a sales mix variance using gross margin percentages

Product	Budgeted sales (€)	Actual sales (€)	Sales variance (€)	Gross variance (%)	Gross margin variance
Balls	60,000	30,000	–30,000	46%	–13,800
Clubs	15,000	10,000	–5,000	36%	–1,800
Bags	5,000	40,000	+35,000	6%	+2,100
Totals	**80,000**	**80,000**	**0**		**–13,500**

In this example overall sales were on target and there was no sales variance. However, the company had been selling fewer of the more profitable products. This is what is referred to as an adverse sales mix variance, and as a consequence of it there is an adverse gross margin variance. This is the reason why having knowledge of gross margins is essential to management.

Generally, a company will wish to sell more of the products that have the highest gross margin percentages. However, there may be production or other constraints that prevent sales volumes or values of products exceeding certain levels.

Example

A company manufactures water filters and chlorinators and wishes to maximize the sales of chlorinators since they are more profitable than filters.

To manufacture these products requires the processes of machining and assembly. However, there are constraints on both of these operations in terms of hours available. There are also limits on the maximum level of sales for both products. A summary of the position is given below:

	Filters	*Chlorinators*
Machine time	3 hours	3 hours
Assembly time	1 hour	3 hours
Unit contribution	€3	€4
Maximum sales possible	160 units	170 units
	Machine room	**Assembly room**
Maximum time available	600 hours	300 hours

We need to know what sales mix of filters and chlorinators will maximize profits subject to the production constraints and sales limits. We can do this with some simple algebra.

Solution:

Let 'x' be the quantity of filters made and sold
Let 'y' be the quantity of chlorinators made and sold

The constraints are:

Machine room: $3x + 3y \leq 600$ hours (because machine room hours must be less than 600)
or $x + y \leq 200$ hours
Assembly room: $x + 3y \leq 300$ hours (because assembly room hours must be less than 300)
Sales of filters: $x \leq 160$ units (because sales of filters must be less than 160)
Sales of chlorinators: $y \leq 170$ units (because sales of chlorinators must be less than 170)

The object is to maximize the overall contribution within the constraints: Maximize the value of $3x + 4y$ but subject to the constraints of:

$x + y \leq 200$
$x + 3y \leq 300$
$x \leq 160$
$y \leq 170$
$x \geq 0$
$y \geq 0$

The mix that will maximize contribution can be found through the following formulae:

$x + 3y = 300$
$x + y = 200$
$2y = 100$ (by subtraction)
$y = 50$ (100/2)
$x = 150$ (by subtraction 200–50)

Therefore the optimal sales mix is:

150 filters
50 chlorinators

Working out an optimal sales mix can be done by trial and error using a spread sheet or constructing a simple linear programme chart. This is shown in Figure 6.3 below.

FIGURE 6.3 Linear programme chart showing optimal sales mix

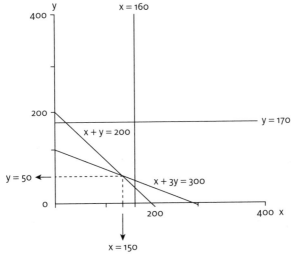

The optimal point is where the lines $x + y = 200$ and $x + 3y = 300$ cross within the constraint lines of $x = 160$ and $y = 170$.

At this point $x = 150$ and $y = 50$

The optimal sales mix is 150 filters and 50 chlorinators

Using simple linear programming techniques to determine optimal levels of sales mix volumes is something your finance department will advise you on, and the above is a guide to the principal methods they will use. In real life the problem can be more complicated and many finance specialists will use computer-simulation programs that can run through many scenarios quickly and are ideal for carrying out sensitivity analysis.

Summary

In this chapter we have covered the basics of product costing and have discussed the merits of marginal costing and full absorption costing. We have seen how marginal cost information can be used to solve sales-volume-mix problems and how cost information can help with sales price determination. A selling price is determined by market forces including the value to a customer and competitive activity. Comparing selling prices that are achievable with cost information can help a company decide whether it is likely to make the required profit from selling a particular product. It might also give some insight into competitors' profitability. There may be occasions where a company lacks accurate market information regarding possible selling prices for a particular profit. In cases like this, a company that believes its costs and operations are efficient might find cost information useful in price determination and also in analysing competitor strategies.

Setting selling prices is an art that requires a combination of market research, competitive analysis and accurate cost information. A structured approach to cost information will help a company make better price decisions and explore alternative strategies.

CHAPTER SEVEN

SETTING SELLING PRICES AND MARKETING STRATEGIES

In the previous chapter we explored costing and some basics of selling prices. In this chapter we will look at a price setting process and some high-level marketing strategies. Since this is a text on financial management we will not stray too far into the area of marketing but will just cover a few essentials that are related to costing and pricing.

For the purpose of this chapter we will define cost and price as being:

- Cost = the costs of production and of bringing a product to market.
- Price = the price that a customer pays for a product or service.

Cost tends to be more internally focused and price has more of an external focus. A process for price determination showing how both internal and external factors are related is given in Figure 7.1.

The steps normally involved in price determination are listed below:

1 Prepare product prime cost estimates for direct materials and direct labour used in manufacturing the product or in providing the service.
2 Calculate the work's cost, which will include the prime costs plus the indirect costs of production overheads.

FIGURE 7.1 Price-determination process

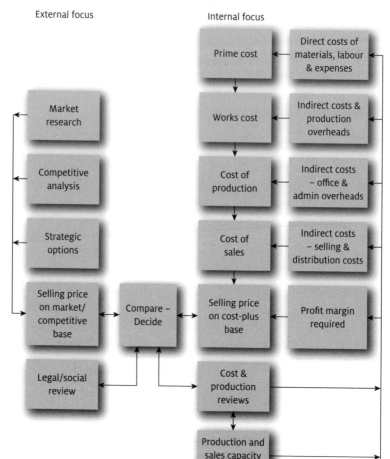

3 Calculate the total cost of production by adding indirect costs of administrative and office overheads to the work's cost.

4 Calculate the cost of sales by adding selling and distribution costs to the cost of production.

5 Decide upon the profit margin required.

6 Calculate the 'cost-plus' selling price by adding the required profit margin to the cost of sales.

7 Determine the market selling price through market research, competitive analysis and looking at strategic options available. Consider marketing strategies – offensive–defensive and rationalization strategies – and factor these into the market selling price.

8 Compare the externally and internally derived prices. Consider the legal and social aspects of both sets of possible prices. Review costs, production capacity and sales mix options.

9 Feed costs review information back into product costs where appropriate.

10 Review all costs and reset internal prices if feasible.

11 Agree on final selling price.

This is an iterative process that will give the best possible chance of getting the right price to achieve sales targets.

There are many factors that determine selling prices. These include:

- customer inertia and reluctance to move;
- the value a customer places upon a relationship;
- time and urgency;
- convenience;
- economic climate;
- perceived quality;
- perceived value;
- unique attributes;
- brand;
- geography;
- competitive strategies;
- marketing strategy – expansion, new market, leader, follower, niches.

These are largely the province of the marketing department and I just mention them briefly here. Marketing strategies and market analysis are outside the scope of this financial management text. However, the effect of marketing strategies on prices is of interest to us and we will consider three major categories.

- offensive;
- defensive;
- rationalization.

Offensive strategies

- Expansion: Open new branches and channels. *Price to win* new business.
- Penetration: Try to win new customers in existing markets and increase/extend existing customer purchases. Differentiation. *Price competitively.*
- Challenger: Being innovative and selling new ideas. Seize new opportunities and outsell competitors with quality and *keen prices.* Take on higher-risk business at potentially *higher prices.*
- Leader: Sell at very keen/*best prices.* Increase distribution network. Increased advertising.

Defensive strategies

- Follower: Take lower risks and possibly accept *lower prices.*
- Niches: Specialize and perhaps obtain *better prices.*

Rationalization strategies

- Cost reduction: Cut costs. Have the ability to sell at *lower prices.*

We can see from the above that whichever strategy is adopted will have an effect on selling prices.

Pricing strategies

Pricing strategies are often considered under the categories outlined below.

Competitive pricing

This is where prices are set with consideration to competitors' product prices. A product may be totally distinctive, have perishable distinctiveness or have little distinctiveness from the competitors' products. Clearly if there is little that distinguishes your product from the competition, then your price may have to track competitors' prices more closely.

Creaming or skimming

This strategy is often used to gain high profits from early adopters of new products and technology. It involves selling a product at a high price, maybe sacrificing some volume but obtaining high margins and perhaps setting higher price expectations. It may be used in an attempt to recover research and development costs.

This strategy can be used only for a limited time; to win greater market share a seller would use other pricing tactics.

Cost-plus pricing

We have discussed at some depth various costing methods and the need for accurate cost information to see how selling prices will contribute to profits. Cost-plus pricing, where prices are set from costs, may have some use when there is no market information but generally has the significant disadvantage of not taking into account market intelligence.

Loss leader

This is where a product is sold at a low price in order to encourage the sale of other profitable products.

Limit pricing

This is a price set by a company with a monopoly in order to discourage new entrants into a market. It is illegal in many countries. The monopolistic company sets a low enough price to discourage a new entrant from entering the market.

Market-researched pricing

This is where prices are set in accordance with market research data.

Penetration pricing

To help penetrate a market, a price may initially be set at a low level.

Price discrimination

This is the practice of setting different prices for the same product in different segments of a market. Examples of this may be age-related pricing or setting different prices at different times, as is often the practice with railways.

Predatory pricing

This is just a term for aggressive pricing to drive out competitors. It might be illegal in some countries.

Premium pricing

Some buyers believe that a high product price equals a high quality. Some sellers will exploit this and price at a premium accordingly.

Contribution-margin-based pricing

We have covered this already in some depth in the previous chapters. It is pricing based on the maximization of contribution (selling price less variable cost). It is a method of comparing the contribution that various products make.

Psychological pricing

This is the practice of pricing to have a psychological effect on a buyer. It is believed, for example, that goods priced at €4.99 will sell more volume than if they were priced at €5.00.

Price leadership

The situation where a company is able to take the lead with prices and competitors fall in line and follow.

Dynamic pricing

A mechanism that has the ability to change prices constantly in response to market dynamics and fluctuations. This will normally be carried out using a computer program that tracks competitors' prices and adjusts your own prices accordingly within pre-set parameters. This process is more suitable to fast-moving commodities.

Target pricing

This is a method where a selling price is calculated to provide a specific return for a specific volume of production. Target pricing may be used most by power and utility companies, where capital investment is high.

Absorption pricing

This is a method of cost-plus pricing that aims to recover all costs attributed to a product on a fully absorbed cost basis plus any possible profit.

High–low pricing

Pricing core products high, with lower promotional price offerings to bring customers in when it is hoped they will purchase the high-priced products.

Premium decoy pricing

Setting the price of one product high so as to make another product seem a bargain. For example, some antique dealers may have a quality item priced very high hoping to make low-value items seem like bargains.

Value-based pricing

This is where a selling price is based on the value to the customer.

Marginal-cost pricing

Selling with consideration to the gross margin. For example, if a product has a total fully absorbed cost of €3 and a variable cost of €2, a company may decide to still sell at only €2.50 since this would still make a contribution to the fixed pool of costs of 50p. In other words it is better off with this sale than without it. Of course, ultimately selling prices need to cover all costs but a contribution is better than nothing at all.

Inertia pricing

Pricing on the basis that existing customers can't be bothered to change or think it is too expensive to change suppliers.

Summary

Setting selling prices is one of the most important tasks undertaken by the executive team. It requires a deep knowledge of the external (market) and the internal factors that affect the decision. Once decided upon, prices need to be carefully monitored in light of sales results and marketing strategies adopted.

In this chapter we have considered some principal pricing strategies, their interface with marketing strategies, costs and some broad legal issues. Whilst selling prices are driven by market forces and not internal costs, a knowledge of product costs is essential to ensure that sales prices produce required returns. If they do not then cost information can provide a guide to where remedial action might be taken. However, it is worthwhile remembering that, for example, a 10 per cent increase in selling prices has a greater positive effect on the bottom line than a 10 per cent decrease in costs. This might seem obvious but it is often forgotten!

Fixing a selling price is not something that a marketing director can do in isolation. It requires close collaboration among the finance director, the sales director and the marketing director. Understanding the value of a product to a customer and the value of any unique selling points or product differentiation is key, and this value information needs to be compared with internal product cost information.

A customer will place a value on a product or services based upon the perceived value to the business, the return that can be made from investing/buying the service, quality, competitive prices and the availability of the product. In the case of some products or services a customer may also place a value on an ongoing relationship with a supplier. An experienced sales or marketing director should know how to maximize selling prices and volumes within a territory, and the consequences of expected selling prices not delivering margin expectations will be something that needs to be resolved with the finance director and the executive team. For example, it may be decided that a higher price can be obtained with an investment in marketing or PR.

Market conditions constantly change and the pricing policy needs to provide the flexibility to respond to these changes. This is where marginal cost information can be very useful in order to see what effect a change in selling price has on the contribution to fixed costs and profits. Failure to react quickly and respond to changing market conditions will result in a loss of sales. A sales director needs to have sufficient flexibility in pricing within certain parameters to be able to close deals without having to revert back each time to the executive team whenever s/he hits a price problem with a competitor. Sales directors need to know the contribution at different price levels and have the power to negotiate to some degree.

There are many factors that affect selling prices and a business needs to be able to react quickly to market conditions. Three of the most important are value to the customer, competition and cost.

Case 12 in Chapter 16 (page 229) gives a practical illustration of cost and selling price decisions.

CHAPTER EIGHT

INVESTMENT APPRAISAL

Organizations make investments with the expectation of gaining future income. Investments may take the form of capital or revenue expenditure. This chapter examines how companies decide which investments to make and looks at the major techniques for investment appraisal.

Relevant cash flow

Before we start any detailed analysis of investment opportunities it is necessary to understand what cash flow is relevant in investment appraisal. Only costs and income benefits that arise as a consequence of the decision under evaluation are of interest to us when evaluating an investment. Examples of relevant costs are:

- opportunity costs (the cost of a lost opportunity resulting from taking an alternative course);
- incremental costs incurred as a result of undertaking the new investment;
- additional taxation arising from the opportunity;
- additional working capital required to undertake the opportunity;
- additional direct/prime costs;
- additional selling and distribution costs;
- new infrastructure costs;
- additional staff costs;
- any other expenditure arising from the proposed investment.

Examples of relevant benefits are:

- additional sales revenue;
- savings in operating costs;
- income from the sale of assets;
- improved customer retention;
- staff retention;
- existing customers extending business;
- any other benefits arising from the proposed investment.

Only costs and benefits that are relevant should be taken into account. For example past costs already incurred are irrelevant.

Example

A boatyard has the opportunity to buy a new moulding for €400,000 to replace an old moulding that originally cost €120,000 and has a scrap value of €6,000. The new moulding would enable annual production to be 100 boats that would sell at €3,000 each.

The production cost of each boat is:

Direct materials (GRP and resins)	€600
Direct labour	€400
Fixed costs allocated	€500 (Fixed costs do not change with production levels or with the acquisition of a new moulding)

The contribution for each boat sale is €2,000 (being €3,000 – €600 – €400).

The new moulding has a life of five years and a scrap value after then of €20,000. It also requires additional skilled operatives for 1,000 hours per year costing €20 per hour. The relevant cash flow is:

Year 0	Purchase price	−€400,000
Years 1–5	Contribution 100 boats @ €2,000	+€200,000 per year
Years 1–5	Skilled operatives 1,000 @ €20	−€20,000 per year
Year 5	Scrap value new machine	+20,000
Year 5	Scrap value old machine	+€6,000

It is this relevant cash flow that will be used to appraise the investment. The original cost of the old moulding is a past cost and is not relevant to the decision so it is ignored. The benefit of €6,000 for scraping the old moulding has been taken into account since the old moulding could have continued to be used.

Pay-back period

This is the most simple method of investment appraisal and is widely used. It simply calculates the time (normally years) that is taken for the opportunity to pay back the initial outlay.

In the above example the initial outlay was €400,000 and there were two relevant scrap values amounting to €26,000. This means that the net outlay was €374,000 (€400,000 − €26,000). The net income from the project is €180,000 per year (€200,000 − €20,000). Therefore, the payback period will be 2.1 years (€374,000/€180,000). It will take approximately two years and a month for the returns on the project to pay back the net investment. Since the mouldings last five years this would seem to be a good investment, if the sales volumes are actually achieved.

$$\text{Pay back period} = \frac{\text{Net investment}}{\text{Benefits}}$$

$$\text{Pay back period} = \frac{374,000}{180,000}$$

$$\text{Pay back period} = \textbf{2.1 years}$$

Pay-back analysis can be used to compare different projects to help decide which one is the best.

Example of the comparative pay-backs for three projects:

	Project 1 €000	Project 2 €000	Project 3 €000
Year 0 Initial investment	120	120	150
Year 1 Profits	40	30	30
Year 2 Profits	40	30	30
Year 3 Profits	40*	30	30
Year 4 Profits	5	30*	30
Year 5 Profits	0	30	30*

Project 1 pay-back period is three years.

Project 2 pay-back period is four years.

Project 3 pay-back period is five years.

Purely on the basis of pay-back, Project 1 has the advantage.

However, the pay-back period does not take account of cash flows outside the pay-back period; this is its weakness.

Although Project 1 has the fastest pay-back, Project 2 produces the greater profit since its income stream runs longer.

Pay-back analysis is a useful rule of thumb as long as one is mindful of its weakness and considers also cash flows beyond the pay-back period.

Return on capital

Also known as return on capital employed (ROCE), this method of investment appraisal measures the percentage earned against the cost of an investment. ROCE is often measured as the percentage average profits are of the average investment.

$$\text{ROCE} = \frac{\text{Average profits}}{\text{Average investment}}$$

Example

A company invests €90,000 in a project that has no residual or scrap value at the end of the project. Income is €15,000 per year for Years 1 to 4 and €10,000 per year for Years 5 to 10.

$$\text{Average earnings per year} = \frac{(4 \times €15,000) + (6 \times €10,000)}{10 \text{ years}}$$

Average earnings per year = €12,000 per year

$$\text{ROCE} = \frac{€12,000}{€90,000} \times \frac{100}{1}$$

ROCE = **13.3% per year**

ROCE can be calculated using several definitions for profits or investments, and may use different combinations of these. For example the calculation can use average profits, total profits, average investments or initial investments. Therefore, when comparing the ROCE of different companies make sure you are comparing a like-with-like method.

ROCE is often used when comparing the return on mutually exclusive projects. A major drawback of the ROCE method is that it does not take account of the timing of cash flows. However, it is a simple and easily understood method that can be used in conjunction with other methods as long as its limitations are understood by users.

Accounting rate of return (ARR)

The ARR method compares profits after depreciation with the original investment or average net book values. It is expressed as a percentage.

There are several different ways of calculating the ARR and it is important to know how it has been calculated before using the information for comparative purposes. An example of the formulae is:

$$\text{ARR} = \frac{\text{Average annual profit after depreciation}}{\text{Original cost of investment}}$$

A weakness of the ARR is that it does not take into account the timing of cash flows, unlike the discounted-cash-flow method, which is explained below.

Discounted-cash-flow and net present value

These are the principal and most widely used methods of investment appraisal because they take into account the timing of cash flows. Money changes value over time and the discounted-cash-flow technique takes account of this. Two methods that use discounted-cash-flow are the net present value and the internal rate of return. We will explore these methods in this chapter.

Future values

The future value of a project is:

$$FV = PV(1+r)^n$$

FV = Future value
PV = Present value
 r = the compound rate of interest
 n = the period

For example, the future value of €3,000 invested for three years at a rate of 4 per cent per year is:

$$FV = €3,000 \ (1+0.04)^3$$
$$FV = €3,000 \times 1.125^*$$
$$\mathbf{FV = €3,375}$$

*(note: 1.125 can also be found in compound interest tables under 3YR/4 per cent (see Appendix 2). It can also be calculated using the y^x key on your financial calculator.

Therefore, if we invest €3,000 for three years @ 4 per cent per year, it will grow to €3,375.

Present value

Using the above example, it is obvious that the present value of the €3,375 must be €3,000. I will now show you how to calculate this.

If the future value is: $\quad$ FV = PV $(1+r)^n$

then the present value (PV) must be: $\quad$ $PV = \dfrac{FV \ 1}{(1+r)^n}$

$$PV = \frac{\text{€}3,375 \times 1}{(1+0.04)^3}$$

$$PV = \frac{\text{€}3,375 \times 1}{1.125}$$

$$PV = \text{€}3,375 \times 0.8889*$$
$$\mathbf{PV = \text{€}3,000}$$

Note: 0.8889 can also be derived from discount tables: YR3/4 per cent.

Therefore, the present value of €3,375 received in three years' time when interest/inflation rates are 4 per cent is €3,000.

You should now understand present value and future value and how to calculate them. Make sure you have a firm grasp of this before moving on to the next section.

Net present value

We have shown above how to calculate the present value. We will now show how to calculate the net present value of a stream of cash flow spread over a number of years. This is best explained by means of a simple example.

Example of net-present-value calculation

A company has the opportunity to make an investment for €400,000 that would yield the following income stream:

Year 1	€150,000
Year 2	€170,000
Year 3	€155,000

If the company has a cost of capital of 5 per cent per year, should it undertake the project? (Note: The cost of capital is explained more fully in Chapter 14.)

To answer this question, calculate the sum of the present values using the 5 per cent discount factors provided by the discount tables below.

Year	Cash flow	5% discount factor	Present value
0	−€400,000	1.000	−400,000
1	+€150,000	0.952	+142,800
2	+€170,000	0.907	+154,190
3	+€155,000	0.864	+133,920
			NPV +30,910

To obtain the present value for each year we multiplied the cash-flow value by the discount factor (obtained from the discount tables). We then totalled the present value column to give us the net present value (NPV). Since this is a positive figure (+€30,910), the yield provided is greater than the company's cost of capital. Therefore, on the basis of NPV the project should be undertaken.

Had the NPV been a negative figure the project would not have yielded a return greater than the cost of capital and, on the basis of NPV criteria, it would not be undertaken.

Discount tables (used for the calculations above)

Years	Discount rates					
	1%	2%	3%	4%	5%	6%
1	.990	.980	.971	.962	.952	.943
2	.980	.961	.943	.925	.907	.890
3	.971	.942	.915	.889	.864	.840
4	.961	.924	.888	.855	.823	.792

For example, the discount factor in Year 2 for a 5 per cent discount rate is 0.907.

The above example assumes that the future income streams are certain. If this is not the case, then allowance can be made by reducing the income streams before discounting by their probability factor. For example, if an income stream of €400,000 was only 95 per cent certain to be realized, then a value of €380,000 (400,000 × 95 per cent) might be used.

The internal rate of return (IRR)

The internal rate of return (IRR) is the discount rate that produces a zero NPV. If the IRR is greater than the company's cost of capital, the project should be undertaken using this criterion. The IRR is an easily understood measure but it does not demonstrate the relative size of projects. However, it is widely used.

Calculating the IRR by simple interpolation

Example

A company has identified an opportunity costing €1,350,000 with the following income stream:

Year	Cash flow
1	+€700,000
2	+€750,000

It has a cost of capital of 3 per cent.

What is the IRR and should the company undertake the project?

Solution

Year	Cash flow (€)	4%	PV (€)	5%	PV (€)
0	−1,350,000	1.000	−1,350,000	1.000	−1,350,000
1	+700,000	0.962	+673,400	0.952	+666,400
2	+750,000	0.925	+693,750	0.907	+680,250
			NPV +17,150		**NPV −3,350**

Steps

1 By experimentation, find the discount rates that give a positive NPV and a negative NPV when applied to the cash flow. In this case you will find that these are 4 per cent and 5 per cent.

2 A 4 per cent discount rate gives a NPV of +€17,150.

3 A 5 per cent discount rate gives a NPV of −€3,350.

4 The internal rate of return must, therefore, lie between 4 per cent and 5 per cent.

5 Using interpolation we can see that a 1 per cent move has resulted in a −€20,500 change in NPV. The move from +€17,150 to −€3,350 is −€20,250.

6 To move from +€17,150 to zero would require the following discount rate:

4 per cent + (5 per cent−4 per cent) × (€17,150/€20,500)

= 4 per cent + 0.837

IRR = 4.837 per cent.

Proof

Using the discount rate formulae DR = $1/(1+i)^n$ we have:

4.8370 per cent

Year	Cash flow (€)	Discount factor	PV (€)000s
1	−1,350,000	1.000	−1,350
2	+700,000	0.954	+668
3	+750,000	0.909	+682
			NPV 0

A discount rate of 4.837 per cent will produce a zero NPV.

This means that the internal rate of return is 4.837 per cent.

Since the IRR is greater than the company's cost of capital of 3 per cent, the project should be undertaken on the basis of this criterion.

(Note: The IRR can also be calculated using a quadratic equation or using a computer program. See also Figure 8.1)

FIGURE 8.1 Internal rate of return graph

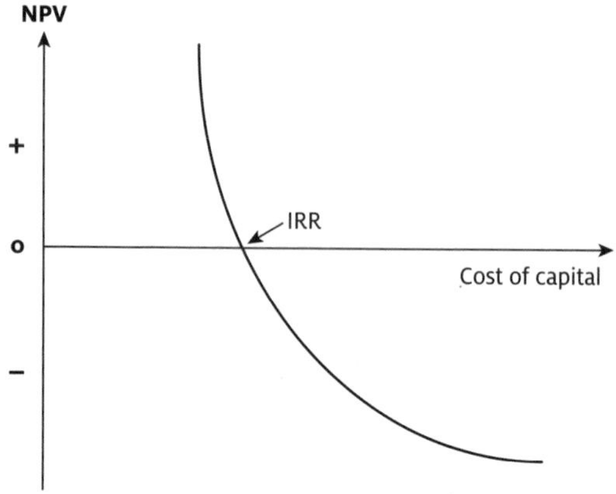

We can plot the range of positive and negative NPVs at different costs of capital to determine the point of IRR.

Capital rationing

A company may have to choose which projects it can undertake within the constraints of its capital and other factors. Projects may be capable of being only partly completed (divisible) or they may have to be completed in total or not at all (not divisible).

When deciding which projects to complete, a company will seek to maximize the overall return subject to the constraints of capital rationing.

Example

A company has three project opportunities (A, B and C). They are divisible and details are listed below. It has €3,000,000 to spend and requires a minimum return of 25 per cent. How should the company prioritize its spend?

	Project A €000s	Project B €000s	Project C €000s
Cost	1,000	2,000	500
NPV	400	1,000	215
NPV as % of cost	40 per cent	50 per cent	43 per cent

All projects exceed the required minimum return of 25 per cent. Clearly Projects B and C provide the highest returns and the company will wish to maximize these. Since the projects are divisible the solution will be:

Project Priority	Investment (€000s)	NPV (€000s)
B	2,000	1,000
C	500	215
A	500	200 (400 × 500/1,000)
	3,000	1,415

The company has spread its €3,000,000 across the three divisible projects in the priority of their returns on investment with the highest first to maximize the overall return to €1,415,000.

Had the project not been divisible then the position would be very different.

Project Priority	Investment (€000s)	NPV (€000s)
B	2,000	1,000
A	1,000	400
	3,000	1,400

Were the projects not divisible the company would maximize its return by choosing Projects B and A. This assumes that it wished to use up all of the capital available.

Summary

In this chapter I have explained some principal methods of investment appraisal used by organizations that wish to maximize the return on their investments. The principal techniques include:

- pay-back period;
- net present value;
- internal rate of return;
- capital rationing analysis.

These are the techniques that are most frequently used in profit-making organizations. However, not all organizations simply seek to maximize returns on investments. They may be seeking to satisfy a broader range of stakeholders' demands.

In any analysis, each variable factor used has a set of underlying assumptions and sensitivities. These may change and in most investment appraisal analysis it is wise to also undertake a sensitivity analysis. This is simply accomplished by taking out one variable factor value and replacing it with another value. Then running the case through again to see what the result is. This can be done a number of times, replacing only one variable at a time in the original appraisal. It is then possible to see how sensitive an analysis finding is to changes in each variable.

Socio-economic, legal, environmental and a whole load of other factors apply to all investment decisions, as well as the financial analysis I have described in this chapter. In addition the effects of taxation should be included in project cash flows.

The methods described are those used most commonly in business investment-decision making. For example, we can put a value on cash flows and look at the probability/sensitivity of underlying assumptions and will readily use this information in a 'dashboard' style of approach to management. However, some may argue that this approach is a little blunt in that management teams have options to change things at the start and as they go along. Real option analysis attempts to apply certain option valuation techniques to capital budgeting and, whilst this is an area beyond the scope of this text, you might want to search for this on the web since it is an interesting concept.

CHAPTER NINE

FINANCE, FUNDING AND WORKING CAPITAL

Finance and working capital

In this chapter we will explain how to choose the correct type of finance and working capital and why this is an important strategic decision. We will discuss short-term funds, long-term funds, equity, gearing, capital structures, leasing, export finance, hedging, managing bank relationships, venture capital and managing interest-rate risk.

A company needs to ensure that it has sufficient finance and working capital to achieve its strategic and operational goals. It is not enough to just make profits. A company needs cash and funds for its short- and long-term needs. Many profitable companies have run into trouble because they do not have sufficient cash. The term 'overtrading' refers to a situation were a company trades at a level beyond its cash and financial resources and cannot pay its debts as they fall due.

A company will have both short-term and long-term funding requirements. These requirements should always be matched with the correct type of funds as follows:

- Use short-term funds to provide for short-term needs such as stocks and debtors.
- Use long-term funds for long-term financial needs such as property purchases, vehicles, plant and equipment, and other capital needs.
- Never use short-term funds for long-term needs. An example of what can happen if you do this is given in Case 1 of Chapter 16 (page 205).

Short-term funds are where the provider has made no long-term (more than one year for example) commitment to provide the funds. Long-term funds are where the provider has agreed to provide the funds for a term of more than one year.

Examples of short- and long-term funds are provided below:

Short-term funds: overdrafts, short-term loans, invoice finance, trade credit, managing stocks

These sources of funds should only be used for short-term needs such as the purchase of stocks or providing credit.

Bank overdrafts

These are normally repayable on demand. Check the small print on the overdraft loan agreement and you will find that they can be called back in by the bank whenever it feels the need. This is because banks have to comply with certain prudential and balance sheet management ratios. Many companies incorrectly treat their overdrafts as term finance. This can be a huge mistake. For example, one company that was trading very profitably used its overdraft to fund the purchase of a new branch. When its profits fell, the bank called back the overdraft and the company was effectively insolvent. So, never use short-term funds for long-term needs under any circumstances.

An overdraft is a short-term facility whereby a bank allows a customer to draw down on its current account and take the account into a deficit up to an agreed amount for an agreed period of time that is subject to review periodically and also if certain performance criteria have not been met. As discussed, the loan is also repayable on demand. The amount of the overdraft limit will depend upon the credit rating of the borrower. This type of facility is very popular because it provides flexibility and the ability to just borrow the amount that is required.

Features of an overdraft are:

- It is repayable on demand.
- Its limits depend on the customer's credit rating.
- It is flexible in that only the amount required from time to time is borrowed.

- Interest is charged on the amount of the draw down (the overdrawn balance).
- Interest is usually expressed as a percentage over base.
- Interest is only charged on the amount drawn down.
- There is usually a facility/set-up/commitment fee.
- There will be penalty fees for exceeding limits without authorization.
- The facility will usually run for 12 months, subject to reviews.
- The limit set is usually based upon cash-flow analysis and needs.
- The facility limit may be reduced by the bank if it is not 'comfortable' with the borrower's performance.
- The bank may require security.

Security may take the form of a floating charge over all the company's assets. Security will depend on the borrower's credit rating, track record and what is available. However, the bank will seek to protect its position as tightly as it practically can. The bank may also require guarantees.

The purpose of an overdraft must meet those required in the agreement. Typically this will be to cover short-term trading deficits, seasonal fluctuations, to provide a bridge between payments and receipts, or to enable a borrower to take advantage of a specific short-term operational business deal that it cannot currently pay for.

If it is clear to a bank that a customer is using an overdraft for something other than short-term funding, then it will probably want to discuss alternatives.

Short-term loans

These are different from overdrafts. They are loans with a fixed repayment schedule usually for a period of up to two years. The principal sum is drawn down at the start of the period and repaid along with interest according to an agreed schedule.

The advantages of a short-term loan include:

- It is known that the funds are available for the agreed period.
- There is pre-defined repayment schedule.
- The loan is *not* repayable on demand.
- It is easier for the bank and the customer to monitor.
- The bank can see if its risk is being reduced as repayments are made.

Some disadvantages include:

- There may be covenants/conditions that the borrower has to comply with or risk being in default.
- The total funds borrowed might not always be needed, whereas under an overdraft facility only the funds needed are drawn.
- The borrower might be paying interest on funds that are not always required.
- Short-term loans will usually charge interest at a percentage over base rate. There are normally facility fees, penalty fees, covenants and security requirements.

Invoice finance (debt finance)

This is a method of using debtor balances to provide finance. The two main methods of invoice finance, which will be looked at below, are:

- factoring;
- discounting.

In debt finance there are three main parties involved. They are:

- The client: this is the party who is owed money and wants to raise finance on the debt.
- The factor/invoice financier: the provider of finance to the client.
- The debtor: the person who has received value and should pay the client.

Debt finance does have significant benefits when managed correctly. The benefits include:

- An improved cash flow.
- There may be less general administration and ledger work.
- Because cash flow has improved there is an opportunity to obtain better discounts from suppliers for earlier payments.
- It is possible to also arrange insurance against bad debts.
- The earlier realization of sales value enables growth.
- There may be less company management time used up in chasing slow payers.

There are, of course, certain disadvantages and these include:

- The client needs to be fully aware of penalties and be sure that these are manageable.

- When factoring is used, the debtor will be aware that the supplying company is using an invoice financier and this may, incorrectly, be construed as a sign of 'tight' finance. This may be the case in some countries more than in others where the practice of debt finance is not so common.

The amount an invoice financier will advance will depend upon the spread of debt and the quality of the debtors. The greater the spread, the lower the risk. When debt is concentrated into fewer debtors the risk will be greater. Of course, the quality of debtors makes a huge difference. For example, a company that has a local authority as its debtor may be viewed as a lower risk that a company whose debtors are small start-up companies.

Some invoice financiers provide both factoring and discounting whilst others specialize in one or the other. I will describe factoring and discounting in detail below.

Factoring

In this system the actual book debt is sold to the factor/financier. The steps in a factoring process are as follows:

1 The client prepares an invoice to the debtor for value provided.

2 The client sends a copy of this invoice to the financier.

3 The financier will make an advance to the client. This can be up to 90 per cent of the gross invoice value.

4 The financier collects the debt from the debtor.

5 After collecting the debt the financier pays the balance of the invoice over to the client, less charges for the service.

The charges mentioned in 5 above will typically include interest at the agreed rate, an administration charge, which is normally a percentage of the gross invoice value, an arrangement fee and fees for an auditor/debtor survey. There will charges for late payments and bad debts.

The reasons you might consider factoring are to:

- improve cash flow quickly;
- save time and effort in debt collecting;
- use debtor balances to provide funds.

Discounting

Under this system the client retains responsibility for debt collection. The book debts are given as security for an advance. The steps in the discounting process are as follows:

1 The client raises an invoice to the debtor for services provided.
2 The client sends the financier the sales-day book listing.
3 The financier provides an advance to the client of typically up to 90 per cent of the value of new gross debts listed.
4 The client manages the debtor and collection process.
5 The client receives payment from the debtor.
6 This payment received is paid into a trust account.
7 The client receives from the trust account the balance of the receipt from the debtor, less charges.

The charges mentioned in 7 above include a discount rate, a commission fee and the money transfer fee (CHAPS fee).

The reasons you might consider discounting include:

● The client (your company) retains control of debt collection and relationship management.
● The client's customers do not need to know about the invoice discounting facility.
● An auditor engaged by the discounter will undertake regular checks on the sales ledger. This can be a benefit and a useful discipline.
● The client has options as to who is responsible for collecting unpaid invoices by way of either recourse or non-recourse discounting.

Some people consider invoice finance to be short term whereas others view it as medium- to long-term finance. It all depends on the detail in the contract. I have included invoice finance under short-term finance because most of these facilities are subject to short-term (three-monthly) reviews.

When choosing an invoice financier it is often a good idea to obtain a reference from a known client or from your accountant.

Trade credit

The time that creditors allow between the delivery of goods or services and when they expect payment may be a source of short-term finance.

The term is normally between 30 and 90 days and many companies rely on it as a regular source of finance. However, the excessive use of trade credit may have a down side. Disadvantages might include:

- loss of discounts;
- late payment fees;
- damage to relationships and loss of goodwill.

Of course, it will always take time for payments to creditors to be arranged, and trade credit is a source of short-term finance.

Managing stocks

Managing stock levels efficiently will ensure that not too much money is tied up in stocks but that there is always enough stock to meet production and sales needs. It is all about achieving an optimal balance.

The economic batch or order quantity (EBQ) is calculated from the following formula:

$$EBQ = \sqrt{\frac{2cd}{ip}}$$

Where:
c = delivery cost per batch
d = annual demand
i = stock holding cost (as a percentage of value or interest)
p = cost price per item

Example

Crates cost €8 each and are ordered in batches of 400. Demand is 5,000 crates per year The ordering cost is €50 per batch. The stock carrying costs are 11 per cent per year of the cost of a crate. What is the EBQ?

$$c = €50$$
$$d = 5,000$$
$$i = 11 \text{ per cent (or 0.11)}$$
$$p = €8$$

$$EBQ = \sqrt{\frac{2 \times 50 \times 5,000}{0.11 \times 8}}$$

EBQ = 754 crates

FIGURE 9.1 Economic batch quantity

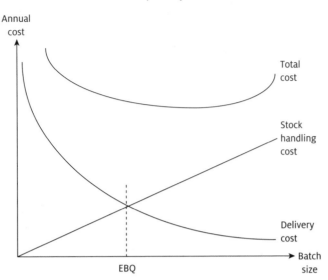

The greater the quantity ordered, the lower the ordering costs per crate (unit). However, the greater the quantity ordered, the greater the stock holding costs. Total costs will be minimized by ordering in quantities of 754. This is illustrated in Figure 9.1.

Leases: short term – long term

Leases are in a class of their own and may be either short term or long term.

A broad definition of a lease is an agreement that gives a right to one person (called a lessee or tenant) to posses property of another person (called a lessor or landlord). The relationship between the lessee and the lessor is called a tenancy. A lease may be for a fixed period but may also be subject to earlier termination. Rent is the term used to describe consideration for the lease. The types of assets commonly leased include vehicles, aircraft, ships, plant, buildings and large mainframe computers.

There are many types of lease and the devil is in the detail. However, the principal types that we will describe are operating leases, finance leases, and sale and leaseback agreements.

Operating leases

These are generally shorter-term leases where:

- The lessor supplies the asset to the lessee.
- The lessor maintains the leased asset.
- The period of the lease is shorter than the economic life of the leased asset.
- At the end of the lease agreement the lessor will either lease out the asset again or sell it.

Finance leases

These are generally for a longer period. Their principal features are:

- The agreement is for most of the asset's expected economic life.
- Most of the risks and rewards of ownership are with the lessee.
- The lessee is responsible for maintenance.
- At the end of the primary period of the asset's useful life the asset has little value because it is worn out or obsolete.
- At the end of the primary (useful) period the lessee might be allowed to continue to use the asset at a 'peppercorn' rent.

Sale and leaseback

A company that owns an asset might sell the asset to a financial institution and lease it back under the terms of a sale and leaseback agreement.

The accounting and taxation rules for the treatment of leases vary between countries. This is a highly specialized area and will affect a decision on which type of lease to adopt. Most large banks will have specialist lease departments for each major class of asset, such as aircraft and vehicles, and will offer advice on which type of lease is an appropriate fit with your business strategy.

Advantages of leasing

There are many reasons why a company may lease. Only some of the reasons mentioned below will apply in any specific case. The general advantages to the lessee of leasing include:

- There may be certain tax relief advantages depending on the country/regime.
- There may be ability to rent an asset that there is insufficient cash to buy.
- A finance lease might be less costly than a loan – a comparison should be made.
- A straight loan may not be available.
- Leasing conserves other lines of credit.
- Up to 100 per cent finance may be available.
- Income can be matched with expenditure.
- Leasing is often convenient.
- It is possible to amortise (spread) the cost of lease fees into and over the life of the lease.

Possibility of fixed-type costs

The advantages of a lease will depend upon the accounting regime and taxation rules applicable in the country in which the company is assessed for taxation.

In the case of an operating lease, the leased equipment might not at the present time have to be shown on the lessee's balance sheet. This will depend upon the accounting regime in the country of the lessee. There may be advantages in having an 'off balance sheet' asset in terms of ratio analysis and analysts' reports. However, international accounting-standards boards are currently debating new rules for lease accounting that would require companies to account on their balance sheets all material assets they have the right to use, and also to include depreciation for those assets. These new lease accounting rules are at this stage in draft form. Whilst the proposed accounting disclosure changes might affect accounting and visibility, it is not yet clear how greatly they might or might not affect strategic financial management decisions. You need to be aware of these proposed changes.

The lessee in a short-term operating lease may avoid having to carry out-of-date or obsolete equipment since the lessor takes this risk.

Lease-or-buy decisions

If a company has enough cash to purchase an asset outright it might still prefer to lease it. Or it might buy it, sell it to a finance company and lease it back again.

The decision as to whether to lease or buy is both a strategic decision and one of financial efficiency. The strategic decision might be concerned with a company's future intentions and the need to conserve cash for a possible future opportunity. The financial efficiency decision will be concerned with getting the best financial deal and making the best use of funds.

Taxation can be a major consideration when comparing lease or buy cash flows. This is because under some tax regimes, for example, the annual cost of an operating lease may be written off as a fully allowable tax expense, whereas in the case of an outright purchase only a part of the cost of the asset may be written off as an allowable tax expense (capital allowances in the UK for example). Therefore, to make a lease-or-buy decision it is necessary, first of all, to compare the net present values (NPVs) of the two alternative methods.

Example

A machine can be purchased for €30,000 or leased for €7,100 per year for five years. Tax depreciation on the purchase price is 25 per cent per year on a reducing balance basis. The lease rental amount can be claimed as a tax-deductible expense each year. Tax is 30 per cent. The after-tax cost of borrowing is 9 per cent per year. Which has the lower net cost, leasing or buying?

Solution
The tax depreciation is shown in Table 9.1.

TABLE 9.1 Tax depreciation

Year		Tax Dep'n (€)	WDV* €
1	€30,000 × 25 per cent	7,500	22,500
2	€22,500 × 25 per cent	5,625	16,875
3	€16,875 × 25 per cent	4,219	12,656
4	€12,656 × 25 per cent	3,164	9,492
5	€9,492 × 25 per cent	2,372	7,119
6	€7,119 × 25 per cent	1,779	5,339

*Written-down value.

The tax depreciation (or capital allowance as it is called in the UK) has been based upon a hypothetical 25 per cent per year reducing balance. These figures will be taken into account in the discounted cash-flow calculations as a tax benefit (Tables 9.2 and 9.3).

TABLE 9.2 NPV of leasing (values in €)

Year	Lease payment	30% tax benefit	Net	Discount factor 9%	PV
1		7,100	7,100	0.917	7,100
2	7,100	2,130	4,970	0.842	4,149
3	7,100	2,130	4,970	0.772	3,837
4	7,100	2,130	4,970	0.708	3,519
5	7,100	2,130	4,970	0.650	3,231
6		2,130	-2,130	0.596	-1,269
					NPV 20,567

NOTES: Lease payments run for five years.
Tax benefits run for Years 2–6.
In the sixth year there is no lease payment but there is a tax benefit.

TABLE 9.3 NPV of purchase (values in €)

Year		Cash flow	30% tax benefit	Discount factor 9%	PV
0	Cost	30,000		1.000	**30,000**
1	Tax allowance	-7,500	-2,250	0.917	-2,063
2	Tax allowance	-5,625	-1,688	0.842	-1,422
3	Tax allowance	-4,219	-1,266	0.772	-977
4	Tax allowance	-3,164	-949	0.708	-672
5	Tax allowance	-2,372	-712	0.650	-463
6	Tax allowance	-1,799	-540	0.596	-322
					NPV 24,081

Comparing just the relevant costs, leasing is the lower cost option:

NPV of leasing: €20,567
NPV of buying: €24,081

Therefore on this basis the company should lease.

However, this is an oversimplified example used to illustrate how discounted cash flows and NPVs can be used in lease-or-buy decisions. There are, in fact, many other variables to consider and take into account, including making an allowance for running costs (which might be different under each scheme), making allowance for scrap value, considering carefully the true economic life of the machine, deciding how each scheme fits with cash-flow management and with strategic plans.

Term funding and long-term finance: optimal gearing, equity funds, ordinary shares, preference shares, debentures, bonds, convertibles, notes, subordinated debt, Eurobonds, commercial mortgages, venture capital, derivatives

Long-term funds and finance are required to finance long-term needs such as fixed assets and term investments. Long-term funds may be equity (shareholders' funds) or debt (term loans).

One of the first decisions to make is whether debt or equity funds are required or whether a mixture of both is needed. The ratio of debt to equity is called gearing and a company with a lot of external debt compared with equity is called a highly geared company.

Optimal gearing–debt/equity ratio

Assessing how much debt and how much equity is required is a strategic decision because the effect that gearing has on the return to shareholders is considerable. When profits are high and interest rates are low, shareholders will benefit from high gearing.

Example of the effect of high gearing on shareholders' interests

A company has a term loan of €800,000 @ 5 per cent interest per year. It has equity (shareholders' funds) of €250,000. Profits before interest and taxation in 2012 are €100,000 and in 2013 they are €200,000. Show the profit after tax and interest that is attributable to shareholders in 2012 and 2013.

	2012 £	2013 £	Increase
Profit before tax and interest	100,000	200,000	100%
Interest (£800,000 @ 5%)	40,000	40,000	
Profit before tax	60,000	160,000	
Tax @ say 30%	18,000	48,000	
Profit after tax available to shareholders	42,000	112,000	167%
Pre-tax return on £250,000 of shareholders' funds	24%	64%	

Note that profits before interest and tax have increased by 100 per cent but the final profits after interest and taxation attributable to the shareholders have increased by 167 per cent. This is because the company is highly geared and interest rates were relatively low. Being highly geared, it has fewer shareholders with whom the final profits need to be shared. The pre-tax return on shareholders' funds has increased from 24 per cent in 2012 to 64 per cent in 2013.

At a time of high profits and low interest rates, the owners of a business might benefit from being highly geared. However, if interest rates were to increase substantially they could see their profits decline. For this reason a company's gearing is subject to close monitoring by the shareholders, who are concerned with their returns, and by the banks who are concerned with their position and the strength of the company they are lending to.

Reaching an optimal level of debt to equity (gearing) will help maximize the value of a company. Gearing decisions are determined by balancing the benefit of the tax deductibility of loan interest (this tends to increase the desirability of external debt and higher gearing) and the higher financial risks associated with high gearing (this tends to moderate the use of debt finance).

Equity funds–ordinary shares

A company issues and sells ordinary shares in order to raise equity funds. This may either be a new issue of shares or a rights issue to existing shareholders.

In most countries ordinary shares will have what is called a nominal value. This is the price at which the shares were first issued and will usually be very different from the price that they are currently trading at on a stock exchange. The dividends that are paid on shares are expressed as a percentage of their nominal value.

Shares are traded freely on a stock exchange at various prices and this has no bearing on the company's financial accounts, where the shares issued will be shown at their nominal value. A company may issue shares at a price that is higher that their nominal value and the difference between the issue price and the nominal price will be shown in a share premium account.

It is the ordinary shareholders who actually own the company, take the risks, enjoy any final profits or suffer losses. Because shareholders take the greatest risk they require the greatest return. Accordingly the cost of equity should be more than the cost of debt.

A company may obtain a listing on a stock market through an initial public offering (IPO), a placing or an introduction:

- An IPO requires the publication of a prospectus and an invitation to the public to buy shares. Sometimes this is referred to as 'going public'.
- A 'placing' is where shares are placed with a small number of specific investors. A placing may cost less and be faster than an IPO. A disadvantage might be fewer shareholders having greater control. When a company first comes onto the market, most stock exchanges will impose a control limit (often 75 per cent) on the maximum number of shares that can be placed.
- An introduction is where a quotation is made on a stock market without the shares being made available in order to obtain a valuation or increase marketability.

The costs of a share issue on a stock market can be substantial; they include advertising and PR, prospectus costs, underwriting costs, listing fees, issuing house fees, solicitors' fees, auditors' fee and a significant amount of internal management time.

When pricing shares, care will need to be taken not to over-price and become under-subscribed or under-price and raise less cash than is possible. The market is normally efficient! When determining a price, consider the price–earnings ratio, current market conditions, the prices of similar companies and the future trading prospects of the company. The time of entry to the market is paramount. Is it a bull or a bear market?

In the case of a rights issue to existing shareholders there should be fewer costs, and there will probably be an expectation by shareholders that they can buy at a price that is lower than the market price at the time of the issue.

Preference shares

These have a preferential right over the ordinary shareholders to profits and to assets on winding-up.

Preferential shareholders, therefore, take a lower risk than ordinary shareholders and on the whole would expect to receive a lower return. Preferential shareholders are normally entitled to a stated level of dividend on their shares and this must be paid before any dividend can be paid out to ordinary shareholders.

Debentures

A debenture is a loan agreement given under the company's seal. It undertakes to provide the debenture holder with a fixed return when the debenture matures. The debenture deed states the rights of the holder. Debentures are used as a long-term debt instrument by governments and large companies.

Debentures will normally be secured over assets of the company by a mortgage deed. A convertible debenture can, after a certain time, be converted into ordinary shares. Different countries have slightly different meanings for the term debenture. In the United States a debenture may refer to a debt security that is not specifically protected by assets. Since there is no universally consistent definition of a debenture it is important to always read the details of the debenture document and understand precisely what it is!

Debentures may carry a fixed charge, a floating charge or no charge at all:

- Fixed charges are over specific assets.

- Floating charges are charges over some or all of a company's assets such that the company can still deal with its assets until the charge actually 'crystallizes' (for example, when the company defaults on the terms in the deed).

- No charge simply means that there is no charge over any assets of the company. These types of debenture are called 'Naked debentures'.

Debentures may be issued at par, at a premium or at a discount. In the UK debentures can be sold and purchased once they have been issued. Market rules vary from country to country. Debentures can be a useful way of raising funds although the constraints imposed by charges might cause inconvenience and a lack of strategic options.

Bonds

These are long-term debts that are issued by a company. Examples are debentures or loan notes. A loan note is a long-term debt (either redeemable or irredeemable) raised by a company. These may be either floating rate, convertible or zero coupon.

Deep-discount bonds

These are bonds that are issued at a large discount against their nominal value. They can be redeemed on maturity at a price that is above par. They would normally, therefore, carry a low rate of interest. Since the holder might get taxed only on the realized gain at maturity these gains could have an advantage over the interest element, which is taxed yearly. It all depends on the taxation regime. If there is a tax cash-flow advantage, then this might be reflected in the rate/price.

Zero-coupon bonds

A zero-coupon bond, as its name suggests, carries a zero rate of interest. They are issued at a discount against their redemption value.

The advantage of issuing these is the opportunity for immediate cash-in with no repayment until redemption.

Convertible loan notes (convertibles)

A convertible loan note incorporates a right to be converted to another form of security at a price and future date; for example, some convertible that may be converted to ordinary shares.

Unsecured notes

An unsecured note is one that is not backed up by any form of collateral. Since lenders have no security they require a greater return.

Subordinated debt

Subordinated debt is subordinate to claims of other debts. This means that lenders have a lower status, carry greater risk and require a greater return.

Eurobonds

Eurobonds are international bonds denominated in a currency that is not native to the country where it is issued. They are traded throughout the world. They are named after the currency they are denominated in. For example, Euroyens. A Eurobond is usually a bearer bond. They are large long-term loans raised by large international companies that have a high credit rating.

Commercial mortgages

The commercial banking arms of the major banks and specialist institutions provide commercial mortgages that give them, as lender, a legal charge over property until the full amount (principal and interest) of a loan has been repaid. The property charged is at risk in the case of default. A commercial mortgage provider might also impose restrictions on the use to which a mortgaged property can be put.

The principal features of a commercial mortgage are:

- Advances are normally up to 75 per cent of an asset's purchase price or valuation, whichever is the lower.
- Loans are normally of €25,000 or more.

- Rates of interest may be fixed or variable.
- Rates may be linked to LIBOR (London inter bank offered rate).
- They are normally for between 2- to 30-year terms.
- Repayments may be monthly or quarterly.
- Mortgages may contain covenants.
- They are often tailored to customer needs with the ability to take repayment holidays.
- They are simple to arrange compared with most other funding methods.

Venture capital

Venture capital organizations will consider providing this type of equity capital to high-growth companies in the expectation of a return through an event such as a company sale of IPO. Venture capital providers are naturally very selective and will require significant equity and control. Because they tend to take on higher risks they expect a greater return.

If you have a sound business proposition then venture capital providers may be interested. Their main sources of new business are start-ups, management buy-outs, exit strategies for business owners and entry into new markets.

Each venture capitalist will have a different area of business specialization and deal size. Deals in the market are often in the €1m to €100m range. The requirements of venture capitalists are explained more fully in the section on 'Financing entrepreneurial thinking' towards the end of this chapter.

Derivatives for hedging

Derivatives are mentioned here because they are relevant to interest-rate risk and currency exchange management in relation to loan contracts.

A derivative is simply an instrument whose value is derived from the value of an underlying asset, commodity, index or some other item. Forwards/futures, options and swaps are all forms of derivative.

A forward/future is a contract to buy or sell an asset at a future date but at a price that is specified today. A forward contract is written directly by the parties themselves, whereas a futures contract is written by an exchange/clearing house where the contract can be exchanged.

An option is a contract that gives the owner the right, but not the obligation, to buy (a call option) or sell (a put option) an asset at a maturity date. There are different types of option. For example under an 'American option' the owner can require the sales to take place at any time up to the maturity date. A 'European option' owner has the right to require the sales to take place on the maturity date but not before. You need to read an option contract carefully to ensure you understand it fully; there are different types.

Export finance: bills of exchange, letters of credit, export credit guarantees

Special types of finance are provided by banks for exporters. Export finance includes bills of exchange, letters of credit and export guarantees.

Bills of exchange

The best definition of a bill of exchange is that given in the Bills of Exchange Act of 1882.

> A bill of exchange is an unconditional order in writing, addressed by one person to another, signed by the person giving it, requiring the person to whom it is addressed to pay on demand, or at a fixed or determinable future time, a certain sum in money to or to the order of a specified person, or to bearer.

International trade finance may be provided by bills, and when a bank discounts a bill it is actually buying the bill at a price that is at a discount from the bill's face value.

Letters of credit

These are documents addressed by a banker to a correspondent bank or agent requesting that an advance be made to the holder and to debit the sum paid to the banker. Various styles of letter of credit are used in export finance.

Export credit guarantees

This is a UK form of insurance against non-payment by overseas buyers. It is provided by the Export Credits Guarantee Department (ECGD).

Using retained earnings as a source of funds

It is, of course, very convenient to simply retain earnings as a source of funds by not paying out dividends. Some companies do just this to the extreme and pay no dividends at all but simply plough profits back into the business, an advantage being that there is no cost of raising capital. In deciding how much dividend to pay, a company will seek to find an optimal mix of finance that minimizes its overall cost of capital. However, finding this optimal mix is a subject of many theories.

The traditional view is that there is an optimal capital structure that will increase the value of the company (see Figure 9.2):

- As gearing increases lenders would assume that a company is more risky and will require a higher return.
- The cost of equity may also rise as gearing increases and financial risk increases.
- The weighted average cost of capital initially falls as the proportion of debt increases but then increases with the rising cost of equity and debt.

There are other views on this subject, including those of Myers and Mailuf and of Modigliani and Miller. There are worth researching on the web if this is a subject that interests you, but for the purpose of this book I just mention them here and take a more simple pragmatic view that each company will have a way of finding what it believes to be its optimal capital structure. It is a strategic decision that takes into account many variables such as future profit expectations, valuations, financial strategy and taxation.

In considering an optimal capital structure and dividend policy a company will need to:

- establish a target for the optimal structure taking into account all constraints, variables and the company's dividend policy;
- use the optimal capital structure to determine the cost of capital;

FIGURE 9.2 A traditional view of the cost of capital

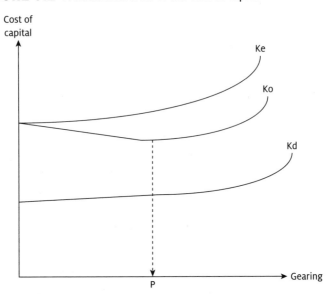

As gearing increases the cost of debt (Kd) eventually increases. The cost of equity (Ke) rises as gearing increases. The weighted average cost of capital (Ko) may initially fall a little as the cost of debt increases, then it will increase with the rising cost of equity and debt. The optimal point of gearing is reached at point 'P'.

- analyse all strategic options and prepare a sensitivity analysis;
- appraise projects using this agreed cost of capital.

A company will be seeking to maximize shareholder wealth; retaining profits will not necessarily achieve this. However, using retained earnings does avoid some costs and also reduces the possibility of a loss of control that might occur with a new issue and change of shareholders.

Bank relationships

We have seen in this chapter that a company has many sources of finance to match its short- and long-term needs. These include internal and external sources.

Many of the external sources of finance are available through banks and financial institutions. A company may need to engage a number of such institutions in order to obtain all of the services and funds it requires. Larger banks tend to offer most services but in many cases, and in order to introduce competition, it may be necessary to engage more than one bank. Also, it sometimes pays not to have 'all your eggs in one basket' and it might be strategically beneficial to separate out services with a number of institutions.

I think that many financial directors will feel that banking relationships can be hard to maintain. Certainly many banks in recent years have viewed customers more on a transactional rather than on a relationship basis. At a lower level, experienced and qualified branch managers have been replaced with less experienced and less qualified staff who are often sales trained and targeted whilst not being empowered to make the sort of experienced judgement calls that a finance director or business manager would require. At the higher end of the corporate banking relationship ladder there has been a high staff turnover and often lack of deep experience.

Many finance directors have different institutions handling each type of transaction. The advantage is that there is more competition and less leverage with any one institution. A disadvantage is that the customer with lots of small relationships is less important to any particular bank and may find it has a lower level of bank attention, trust and goodwill. However, on balance most finance directors want to be in control and do not want to rely on a relationship that may not be reciprocated.

In general I would make the following observations at this point in time regarding bank relationship strategy:

- Banks continue to become more transactional rather than relationship driven. As a result of this some corporate executives may value their bank relationships less than they used to.
- Many customers continue to separate out their services by using different financial providers. In particular more companies than before separate out their money-transmission from their lending bank.
- Many customers pay for stand-by and back-up facilities with an institution other than their principal bank.
- Relationship managers often change and often are not as empowered as a finance director had assumed.
- Depending on a single banking relationship is generally not a robust strategy.

When deciding on which bank to engage it can be helpful to make a list of services required and the potential institutions that can be used, as outlined below.

Service	Institution/Bank/Network
Money transmission and day-to-day banking	Bank A and Post Office Network
Current accounts	Bank N
Long-term loans	Bank C
Short-term loans	Bank N
Overdrafts	Bank N
Working capital finance	Invoice discounter E
Payment services	Bank N
International payments	Bank N
Merchant and investment banking	Bank Y
Foreign exchange dealing	Banks N and C
Money market dealing	Banks N and C
Term investments	Bank XXX

The simple logic behind these theoretical choices is:

- Consider keeping money transmission separate from the bank that provides current account and overdraft so that funds can be diverted to another bank quickly if this is required (refer to Case 5 in Chapter 16, page 213).
- Find the most convenient network for paying in and transmission that is independent from your current account bank. This might be the Post Office Network.
- Look for a strong institution to provide all current account, overdraft, short-term loans, payments and other day-to-day services.
- For long-term loans introduce more competition and consider keeping this away from your current-account provider.

- For working capital finance consider a specialist invoice finance company.
- Get some competition when making foreign currency purchases by asking two or more banks to quote.
- In the case of term and other investments look closely at the credit rating of the institution. Consider spreading risk.
- Consider specialist banks for merchant and investment banking needs.

Having the time and resource to research and build up these multiple banking relationships may be difficult for a small company with a hard-pressed finance director. In the case of a large multinational organization it will be normal to have many banking relationships to obtain best value and for strategic reasons. The balance of power may be more weighted towards the corporates and they can demand a better response and level of service.

Covenants

An important element to a good banking relationship is a thorough understanding of any loan covenants since these are often a source of frustration for businesses (as seen in Case 4 in Chapter 16 page 211).

A loan covenant is a condition that requires a borrower to fulfil certain conditions.

Failure to comply with a covenant may result in a default, with penalties being applied and/or the loan being called in. Covenants may be waived and the loan agreement renegotiated by the lender. This will normally only occur if it is in the lender's interest.

Covenants are generally undertakings given by a borrower as a part of a loan agreement. They require the lender to ensure that the risk to the lender does not increase prior to maturity. They should not be entered into lightly because failure can result in adverse consequences for the borrower. They help increase a bank's control and give advance warning of potential problems.

There are many types of covenants, depending upon the type of business. They may include:

- loan to value ratios;
- interest cover;

- a requirement to keep certain insurance cover;
- agreements to pay all taxes;
- the submission of financial reports;
- maintenance of financial ratios;
- additional lending restrictions;
- dividend payment restrictions;
- restrictions on business ownership and mergers;
- restrictions on changing management.

You can see from the above that a covenant in a loan agreement can put a bank in a position of considerable strength that it may use for its own protection and advantage. Covenants should not, therefore, be entered into lightly.

Financing entrepreneurial thinking and venture capitalists

It is hard to precisely define an entrepreneur but one thing they have in common is an ability to see the future as a different place. They have a vision, ability to innovate and the enthusiasm to make their vision happen. They are the creators of the new ideas needed to create new opportunities and growth.

Few of these new ideas would ever get started without sponsorship and finance. This requires a form of judgement and risk analysis in addition to the financial analysis applied to less ground-breaking ideas and opportunities.

Some entrepreneurs are inventors of entirely new products whilst others have an idea that will use existing technology to achieve a different outcome. Of course, not all entrepreneurs are inventors but certainly they will be promoting a new idea. Compared with an existing product we are talking about shades of grey as far as a financier is concerned. In terms of funding research for new ideas this is often considered as either applied research (where a specific application has been identified) or pure research (where the idea may have benefits that have yet to be linked to an application). All of this 'grey stuff' creates a problem for the financier who uses simple financial analysis alone and is not the sort of risk that most banks will consider. In cases like these the entrepreneur needs to talk with a venture capitalist.

A new idea carries a higher risk. Providers of finance for higher risks require a higher return, and this typically requires an equity investor. Venture capitalists own equity in the companies they invest in and will usually require significant control.

Venture capitalists are understandably very selective in their investment decisions. Typically they will reject the vast majority of proposals that come their way. Their interest will be in very high growth opportunities with a clearly defined exit strategy within a typical time frame of three to seven years. This will need confidence in the entrepreneur. This is extremely important since even a good idea with a weak entrepreneur will not succeed.

A venture capitalist will not just provide capital but will be involved in every stage of the business opportunity from concept to their final exit. This will include:

- idea creation and development;
- start-up;
- business development;
- exit.

The financing stages are typically:

- seed money to help prove the new idea;
- start-up money to fund product development and marketing;
- round one money for manufacturing and sales;
- round two money for finance sales until profitability is reached;
- round three money to assist expansion of the company once it is profitable (this is also called mezzanine finance);
- round four money to assist going public and reaching the exit point.

When looking for a suitable venture capitalist consider their current portfolio. It might help if they specialize and have knowledge of the sector you are in. Also, consider their typical investment size and any regional preferences.

Venture capitalists are rewarded for their work and risk through a combination of management fees and interest/share of profits.

There are alternatives to venture capital, and one of these is 'crowd funding'. This simply means spreading the risk over large numbers of people, each of whom makes a small donation. Online communities make it easy to reach large groups of potential investors at a very small cost.

Interest-rate risk

An organization that either borrows or invests money will be exposed to an interest-rate risk. It may either pay more interest than it expected or receive less interest income than it had hoped for. Interest-rate risk is the sensitivity of profits to fluctuations in interest rates.

As part of its risk and sensitivity analysis an organization should calculate what effect a change in interest rates will have on both profits and cash flow. What effect would a 0.5 per cent change in interest rates have on the company and how likely is this risk? Clearly a company with more variable/floating-rate interest will be more sensitive to changes than one with a higher proportion of fixed-rate contracts. However, as we shall see below, even companies with fixed-rate contracts have an element of exposure!

Interest rates are used by governments and central banks to help control an economy. The rates may fluctuate due to changing economic conditions, yield curves and the structure of rates. Central banks and governments may use interest rates to help control inflation. Case 16 in Chapter 16 (page 236) provides some insight into how governments might use interest rates to control inflation and the risks this creates for some businesses.

Generally, investors want more compensation for losing their liquidity and tying up their cash for a longer term. This means that they want a higher interest rate for investing longer term. This is one

FIGURE 9.3 An interest rate/yield curve

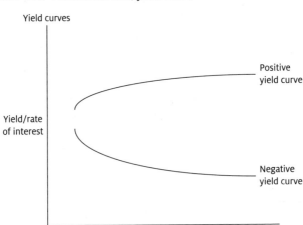

reason why an interest-rate/yield curve might be positive. However, for a variety of reasons a yield curve can also be negative. The shape of a yield curve needs to be understood when selecting a hedging strategy.

Floating or variable rate interest exposure

A company that has a high level of floating-rate debt will be very vulnerable to changes in interest rates. Floating rates change according to general market conditions. The company might find that its customers do not accept price increases in line with changes in interest rates. For example, a customer might have an alternative supplier with a different capital/debt structure that does not need to increase prices when interest rates rise.

Fixed-rate interest

Whilst a company that has a high level of fixed-rate debt might not be so vulnerable to the volatility of market rates it does still have an exposure to changes in rates. For example if the interest rate falls sharply then a company with fixed-rate debt might find that it is not so competitive as a company that has floating-rate debt and can now offer lower prices! This is often overlooked, and the extent to which a company is exposed will depend upon the capital/debt structure of its competitors.

It is a simple matter to determine the degree to which an organization is exposed to interest-rate movements. One method employed is that of 'gap analysis'. This is where assets and liabilities that are sensitive to interest-rate changes are grouped together according to their maturity dates. A 'gap' may occur and this will help identify overall exposure. When preparing a gap analysis, be careful not to ignore 'basis' risk. This is the base rate upon which floating-rate margins are based. For example, some contracts may be based on LIBOR and others may use a different base.

Interest-rate risk management

There are a number of ways of managing interest-rate risk. An organization can use internal methods such as matching or smoothing, or external methods such as derivatives and forward-rate agreements.

Matching is where an organization matches its interest-bearing assets and liabilities so that exposure is offset. Smoothing is where an organization keeps its fixed and floating-rate exposure in balance.

Forward-rate agreements (FRAs) fix an interest rate on future borrowings, thereby hedging risk. FRAs are normally only available on larger loans. The bank will fix the rate of interest for a future date. If the actual rate on that day proves to be higher, then the bank pays the organization the difference. If the actual rate on the day is lower, then the organization pays the bank.

Interest-rate derivatives include futures, options, caps/collars/floors and swaps. A borrower may sell an interest-rate future to hedge against rate rises, and lenders may buy futures to hedge against falls in rates. Interest-rate options grant the buyer the right but not the obligation to deal at an agreed interest rate. 'Caps' set a ceiling to an interest rate, a 'Floor' is an option that sets a lower limit to interest rates and a collar is the simultaneous purchase of a cap and a floor. An interest-rate swap is where two parties agree to exchange interest-rate payments. A fixed-to-floating-rate currency swap is both a currency and an interest-rate swap.

When using any of the external methods of matching interest-rate exposure, your finance director will need to understand the product and be sure that any proposed transactions are authorized by the board and not speculative transactions (unless this is the organization's business).

Financial markets

There are many types of institutions that make up the financial markets. The type of institution you deal with will depend on the type of finance or capital required.

Financial intermediaries

A financial intermediary links lenders (those with surplus funds) to borrowers (those who need funds). The service they provide is based upon aggregation, the economies of scale, risk sharing and maturity transformation. Types of financial intermediary include finance houses, commercial banks and institutional investors.

Money markets

Money markets provide short-term capital. This includes short-term financial instruments and short-term lending/borrowing. The money markets are operated primarily by the banks.

Capital markets

The capital markets provide long-term capital. A stock exchange is a principal capital market and has two main purposes:

- It is a primary market for raising new finance through the issuance of shares or new loan notes.
- It is a secondary market to enable existing investors to sell their investments.

International money and capital markets

These exist for major companies to raise large amounts of finance and include the Eurocurrency Market and Eurobonds.

Summary

Choosing the correct type of finance and working capital is an important strategic decision. In this chapter we have discussed short-term funds, long-term funds, equity, gearing, capital structures, leasing, export finance, hedging, managing bank relationships, venture capital and managing interest-rate risk. Your finance director will be trying to ensure that there is competitive finance available to meet the strategic and operational needs of the company. Key to this is achieving an optimal balance between the lowest cost and the maximum flexibility of finance to support the aspirations of the business.

Choosing the correct bank/s and maintaining a relationship can be challenging for smaller companies, particularly if they do not warrant an experienced and empowered banking executive. Changes in bank ownership and internal bank re-organizations can result in a finance director losing a long-standing relationship with a bank executive who understood the customer's business. Relationships can have enormous value and are worth some investment to maintain. However, many banks and their customers now simply operate on a transactional basis.

Several of the case studies in Chapter 16 demonstrate how things can go wrong between banks and customers and in managing finance generally.

CHAPTER TEN

INTERNATIONAL TRANSACTIONS AND CURRENCY RISK

Banks and other institutions provide a range of services to facilitate, finance and insure international transactions. These include international payments, documentary credits and collections, guarantees, insurance, currency accounts, loans, foreign exchange purchase, currency exchange risk management, hedging and derivatives.

In this chapter I will concentrate of the most common types of foreign transactions. These are:

- buying or selling foreign currency;
- foreign exchange risk management;
- foreign currency accounts;
- export invoice finance.

Buying or selling foreign currency

If you are trading internationally you will probably need to buy or sell foreign currency.

If you are importing you may need to purchase foreign currency to pay for the goods you are importing. For example if you are a UK-based company purchasing yachting equipment manufactured in New Zealand, the manufacturer may require that you pay for the goods in

NZ dollars. Therefore, you will need to purchase the NZ dollars and probably pay for them using your local currency – Sterling.

When approaching your bank to purchase the NZ dollars you will need a destination account. This could be the supplier's account or you might have your own NZ dollar account already set up. If you are regularly trading with NZ you may well have.

The bank will offer you a rate of exchange for NZ dollars against sterling, and there will also be payment/transaction fees. You will, particularly if the payment is a large one, want to obtain competitive quotes. To do this you will need to have dealing lines set up with other banks. This is so that they know who you are and can ensure they get paid.

It is normal to have three dealing lines in place and obtain simultaneous quotations. This may require several staff at the office working together and in close communication.

Once you have accepted the best quote, you will provide payment instructions and the deal is concluded.

Similarly, if you sell goods overseas, or for a variety of other reasons, you might need to sell a foreign currency. This is a similar procedure. Always ensure that you get a good price and obtain competitive quotes.

If you expect to have to buy or sell foreign currency at a future date against your local or some other currency, then you have an exposure to the risk of exchange rates moving either in your favour or against you. We will discuss below how to hedge against such events.

When buying or selling currency it is worthwhile remembering:

- Open dealing lines with a number of providers and read and compare the small print in their terms and conditions.
- When obtaining competitive quotes be sure that you compare like with like. The market changes every second, and if you are to obtain a fair comparison between quotes they will need to be obtained and compared simultaneously. Work out in advance how you are going to do this. Large companies have a treasury operation set up to do this but a smaller company may need to make some special arrangements.
- It is always your responsibility to ensure that the provider of the foreign currency is reputable because your government may not regulate foreign currency trading. Foreign currency trading may provide a vehicle for illegal activity such as money laundering and you need to be sure of whom you are dealing with.

- Obtain a good mix of providers to quote: some banks and some independent currency providers.
- Plan the transaction well in terms of time, staff and having the dealing line in place.
- Indicative rates can sometimes be used to entice a buyer. The real rate may be not so good. Also check for hidden charges.
- Carry out security and status checks on your providers.
- Make sure that you understand the operating procedure for delivery and holding of your currency. Currency you have bought that is pending transfer should be held in a separate holding account.
- You must insist on timely documentation and transaction confirmations.
- You should normally expect better rates for larger transactions.

Foreign exchange risks

A foreign exchange risk can occur whenever there is a mis-match between the currencies in which receipts and payments are made. For example, if a NZ-based company has NZ customers who pay in NZ dollars but has suppliers in the United States who require settlement for their invoices in US dollars, then there is a mis-match between the currencies of receipts and payments. There is an exposure to foreign exchange risk.

Unless the company is in the business of trading and speculating in currency it should seek to either eliminate or manage currency risks. The aim should be to make neither a loss nor a profit from an exposure but to manage the position.

Some of the common causes of foreign exchange risk are:

- making overseas payments for imports that are priced in a foreign currency;
- receiving foreign currency for exports;
- borrowing in a foreign currency;
- investing or depositing funds in a foreign currency;
- having overseas subsidiaries and operations;
- owning property overseas.

Some companies may have both overseas assets and liabilities that, to an extent, match or partially offset each other, thereby reducing their exposure to currency risk. However, in most cases a company will need to develop a plan and strategy for managing its exposure and we will discuss these techniques later in this chapter.

A currency loss/gain can occur on a specific transaction (transactional risk) or on translation (translation risk). Examples of these are given below:

Transactional risk example

A UK company imports superyachts from the United States. The board have approved the purchase of one yacht costing US$825,000. The UK equivalent at the time was £500,000 and this was based on the US$/£ rate at the time of £1 = US$1.65. The approved UK budget was, therefore, £500,000.

The US supplier agreed to hold the price at US$825,000 for six months. When the order was due to be placed the rate of exchange had changed to £1 = US$1.61.

	UK £ Sterling	Rate of exchange	US$
Approved budget	500,000	1.65	825,000
Actual at time of order	512,422	1.61	825,000
Loss on exchange	**12,422**		

Because the rate of exchange has moved against the company, it will require an additional £12,422 in order to place the order and complete the transaction. This will require going back to the board and seeking approval. There are ways of hedging against this type of occurrence that we will discuss later.

Translation risk

When a company has overseas assets or liabilities at the year-end balance date, it will need to convert these into its local currency for financial reporting.

For example, a UK company has a US asset valued at US$300m. The rate of exchange at 31/12/10 was £1/US$1.65 and the rate of exchange at 31/12/11 was £1/US$1.69. The loss on translation will be:

Asset value at 31/12/10 US$300m. Rate £1 = US$1.65   = £181.8m
Asset value at 31/12/11 US$300m. Rate £1 = US$1.69   = £177.5m
Translation loss on 31/12/11   £4.3m

At the point in time (31/12/11) the company would record a translation loss of £4.3m. A few days later the rate could have moved either favourably or adversely.

Economic risks and hidden risks

Economic and hidden risks may occur when a rate of exchange movement in a currency that is not dealt in directly affects competitiveness. For example, a UK manufacturer sells products to a UK customer – on the face of it there is no exchange exposure here. However, what if the pound strengthens against the yen, making imports from a Japanese competitor cheaper to the UK customer? This is one example of an economic risk. There are many other hidden and economic risks, particularly through the supply chain where a local supplier might be sourcing supplies from an overseas company.

Foreign currency accounts

A company that has regular foreign currency assets or liabilities might find it convenient to open a foreign currency account. It can use the account to match or partially match foreign currency receipts and payments, thereby reducing its risk to currency exchange rate exposure. The advantages include:

- a possible reduction in the risks associated with exchange rate movement;
- fewer costs associated with undertaking currency deals;
- convenience;
- an account where overseas customers can deposit payments;
- foreign currency funds available at all times when needed;
- simple to set up and to view balances;
- overdrafts might be possible – subject to credit rating.

There are possible disadvantages, particularly in holding large balances in foreign currencies. Unless you expect to have an offsetting transaction/balance you will increase exposure and risk to exchange rate movements. Some countries might impose exchange controls that could affect your ability to move funds. Then there is the possibility of devaluation. Of course there will be fees involved in opening a foreign currency account and you might be required to maintain a minimum balance.

Opening a foreign currency account is a fairly simple procedure and can be undertaken with most large international banks. Of course, when purchasing funds to deposit in a currency account it is generally beneficial to obtain competitive quotes.

Forward exchange contracts

Future exchange rates are very difficult to predict and if a company has an exposure to a currency exchange risk it might choose to hedge against this by using a forward exchange contract.

A forward contract is simply an agreement between two parties (one of which is usually a bank) to exchange one currency for another currency at a certain rate of exchange at a future date.

Forward contracts have the following principal features:

- They are for the purchase or sale of an amount of a specific currency.
- The exchange rate is fixed at the date of the contract.
- The delivery of the currency is at a specified future date.
- The contract is binding.

Example of a forward contract

A US-based importer contracts to buy goods from a UK supplier for £50,000. The invoice is payable in 30 days' time.

The US importer takes out a forward contract with its bank to deliver £50,000 in 30 days time at a rate of £1/US$1.63.

The US importer now knows that the cost will be US$81,500 (this is £50,000 × 1.63). This deal has provided certainty and the US importer may be able to back this with a US sale, knowing what its costs are. When using the forward exchange market it is usually best to obtain several quotations.

The forward contract has introduced certainty and has enabled the US importer to remove the currency risk. The importer is not a currency speculator and simply wants to remove risk and match currencies.

Of course, the actual rate on the day in 30 days time (the spot rate) could be very different. However, this is not relevant and the company should not be wondering if it has made a profit or loss by taking out the forward contract compared with the spot rate on the delivery day – it has introduced certainty in its normal business transactions and eliminated risk. It would only be interested in taking a position with a view to gain if the directors had authorized such speculation or if speculating on exchanges was in the normal course of business.

Hedging using the money market

A business with a future currency exposure might decide to borrow in its home currency on Day 1 and use the borrowed money to purchase the required foreign currency, which will be deposited in an interest-bearing account until needed. By doing this, the company will have certainty of the exchange rate and be able to eliminate currency risk on the principal amount. It will have earned interest in foreign currency and incurred local interest on its borrowing, and there will be an exchange exposure here. However, over a short period this will be small compared to the exposure on the principal sum. Of course, there may also be differences between the local and the foreign interest rates. This is a useful alternative to buying forward, especially if the company already has an appropriate foreign currency account. In an efficient market there should not be an enormous difference in cost between using this method and using the forward exchange market. It might be worthwhile comparing the costs of this method with forward exchange market quotations.

Currency futures

A currency future is a form of derivative and can be used to hedge against currency risks.

Currency futures are contracts where the 'underlying' is a currency exchange rate. They can be traded in the same way as any other future on the futures exchange markets. They are different from a forward contract, which cannot be traded. They are based on the exchange rates of two markets and are settled in the underlying currency of the futures market. A currency future is a futures contract to exchange one currency for another at a specified date at a price that is fixed on the purchase date. Accordingly these futures are used to hedge against an exposure and, in the case of an organization authorized to do so, they may be used to speculate.

In this book we are only interested in hedging as a tool of financial management.

Some of the principal advantages of currency futures are:

● Transaction costs are often lower than other forms of hedging.
● They are fully tradable.

Some principal disadvantages are:

● They to not allow companies to take advantage of possible future exchange rates as do currency options (discussed later).
● There are only a limited number of currencies available.
● Since futures are tradable, their price may move differently from their 'underlying'.

Example of a futures contract

A US-based company buys wine from a French company for €200,000 payable in 30 days. The US company has decided to hedge against its exposure by using the currency futures market.

Current rates are:

Spot rate	US$0.935/€
Futures rate	US$0.945/€

The rates in 30 days time are:

Spot	US$0.955/€
Closing future price	US$0.960/€

The contract size is €100,000.
Only three-month contracts are available.
The company will need to buy € or sell US$.

The number of contracts it will need to buy is exactly two
(€200,000/€100,000)
The 'tick size' (the smallest unit of movement in the contract price)
is 10.00 (€100,000 × 0.0001)

Opening futures price – buy	0.945
Closing futures price – sell	0.960
'Tick' movement	150

The futures profit is 150 ticks @ say US$10 per tick × 2 contracts =
US$3,000. The net payment is 30 days' time will be:

30 days spot €200,000 @ 0.955	US$191,000
Futures profit	US$3,000
Net	US$188,000

This calculation is for illustrative purposes only, to demonstrate the
principle of how currency futures pricing might work. Each type of
contract needs careful examination by skilled staff experienced in
futures trading. They will need to plot out their understanding with
their adviser before committing to anything. It is exceedingly easy to
make a mistake with this type of transaction!

Currency options

A currency option gives the owner the right but not the obligation to
exchange one currency for another at a future specified date and at a
specified rate. Therefore, an option enables a company to limit its
downside without limiting its gain. Because an option allows for
unlimited gains, some people argue that this part of the deal is a form
of speculation. Because the user of an option is not obligated to buy
or sell, their potential gains are not limited.

Currency options are often traded over the counter between two
parties or on exchanges.

The 'underlying' of an option is the foreign exchange rate. A call
option is the right but not the obligation to buy the underlying. A
put option is the opposite in that it is the right to sell but without any
obligation. A 'strike' price is the guaranteed price chosen by the user/
client. This can be at the money (ATM), in the money (ITM) or out of
the money (OTM). ATM is the market rate, ITM is better than the market

and OTM is worse than the market. Options are not like futures or forwards where the current rate in the market is pre-determined. The client chooses a rate.

A currency option might be appropriate when the future foreign cash flow is uncertain. If the option shows a profit on the delivery date the holder will exercise the option and the net cost will be the cost of the underlying plus the premium less the profit.

Example of a currency options contract

If a £/US$ currency option contract allows the owner to sell £400,000 and buy $600,000 on 31/12/11, the pre-arranged strike price is 1.5000 and the notionals are £400,000 and $600,000. The contract is a call on US$ and a put on £ Sterling.

If on 31/12/11 the rate is 1.45, then the dollar is stronger and the £ Sterling is weaker. The option will, therefore, be exercised. The owner of the option will sell £400,000 at the option price of 1.5 and immediately buy it back at the spot market price of 1.45, thereby making a profit as follows:

$$£400,000 @ 1.50 = \$600,000$$
$$\$600,000 @ 1.45 = £413,793$$
$$\text{Profit} = £13,793 \ (£413,793 - £400,000)$$

Like futures, an option contract can be exceedingly complicated and a company will seek expert advice. It is best to plot out the cash flow and options on a chart, and to ensure they are fully understood and agreed with the financial institution providing advice.

Currency swaps

A currency swap is where parties contract to swap equivalent amounts of currency for a period of time by exchanging debt from one currency to another.

Example

A UK company wishes to invest in the United States and borrows £20 million from a UK bank at 5 per cent. The £20 million will be converted

FIGURE 10.1 Currency swap

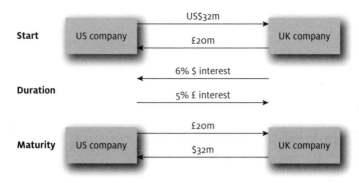

into US\$ at the spot rate of \$1.60/£1. The US investment will yield income in US\$. The UK company agrees to swap the £20 million for \$32m with a US company that now becomes the counterparty to the transaction. Interest is at 6 per cent on the \$32m. The UK company will invest the whole of the \$32m in the United States (see Figure 10.1).

● UK company receives interest on \$32m @ 6 per cent = \$1.92m per annum.
● The UK company gives this \$1.92m to the US company so that the US company can pay its interest.
● The US company passes its interest to the UK company. This will be £20m @ 5 per cent = £1m per annum.
● The UK company pays this £1m over to the bank, its lender.

At the end of the swap period:

● The UK company will pay back the \$32m.
● The UK company receives back the £20m.
● The UK company pays back the £20m to its lender.

Currency swaps require an exchange of interest and principal. They may be used to hedge against a risk.

The principal features of a currency swap are:

● Interest rates are agreed in advance.
● Currency exchange rates are agreed in advance.
● The two parties exchange the principal sums at maturity.

The three types of currency swap are: fixed-to-fixed rate, fixed-to-floating rate and floating-to-floating rate.

Currency swaps may be used to hedge against currency movements for a longer period than is normally possible using forward contracts. Deals are usually for seven years or less, and amounts generally exceed £5 million.

Before a currency swap is undertaken it is necessary to consider the implications for the company's balance sheet. Accounting rules vary from one country to another, but many will require the swap to be treated like a back-to-back loan and shown in full on the balance sheet, thereby affecting balance sheet ratios and analysis.

Invoicing in domestic currency

One very simple way to eliminate currency risk is to get foreign customers to agree to be invoiced in the seller's currency and to settle in this. This simply passes the problem over to the foreign customer and may well be acceptable to them, depending on their own exposures and trade. For example it may help them offset another position. The same can apply to imports. It is always worth asking if a foreign customer or supplier would accept invoice/settlement in your own local currency. Many will!

Advance payment

To obtain an acceptable and certain rate of exchange it may be possible to settle with the foreign party in advance. However, this will replace an exchange risk with a delivery risk.

Matching

A company should always try to match its foreign currency receipts with any similar currency payments to eliminate or partially eliminate currency exposure. This is probably more easily done through the operation of a foreign currency account.

Intra-group trading

Subject to the laws, regulations, taxation implications and accounting conventions of various countries, it might be possible to net off debit and credit balances on intra-company trading so that only net balances are paid. This will reduce foreign exchange exposure and transaction costs. However, it can be a minefield of taxation and other regulations; beware of falling foul of them.

Export invoice finance

Many banks offer a range of export invoice finance facilities. For example:

- Up to 85 per cent of an export finance invoice can be made available the working day after billing. This can help a company offer open terms to an overseas customer, helping it compete with local suppliers.
- Many global banks provide sales ledger management services with collections and cash allocation processes through their own networks and through corresponding invoice finance providers abroad. They also provide linguists.
- Some banks also provide overseas customer credit protection. This can be compared to the ECGD service described previously.
- Larger global banks will also provide major customers with a dedicated relationship manager who can advise and assist with complex international transactions.

Single Euro Payments Area Direct Debit Scheme

The Single Euro Payments Area Direct Debit Scheme (SEPA DD) was launched in 2009 and may be nearing the point of mandatory implementation in a few years' time. SEPA DD is a single and convenient way to accept and make payments across European countries. For example, the scheme enables a UK company to organize all euro payments from a single domestic bank account. This will improve cash control and money management, making business transactions throughout Europe much simpler. SEPA DD is designed to make business throughout Europe a lot easier and it will, no doubt, enable more companies to consider growing their business in Europe. Your bank will advise you further and you will be impressed with how easy and straightforward things have become.

Summary

International trading can expose a company to considerable risk. The purpose of this chapter has been to explain some of the more common ways of hedging against these risks.

The methods and services provided by the banks enable companies to choose a hedging facility appropriate to their type of risk. First, however, it is necessary to identify the direct and more obvious transactional and translation type risks, whilst not forgetting the more hidden and economic risks. Then, it is also necessary to remember that, unless you have a mandate otherwise, you use these services to hedge and insure against risks and not to speculate. Speculation on the currency market is for currency dealers. Speculators are, of course, a necessary part of the market; however, unless foreign currency is your business why would you speculate in it? This might seem obvious but many companies get confused between hedging and speculating: between covering a position and taking a position. Case study 2 in Chapter 16 (page 207) demonstrates speculation and hedging.

A company should not leave itself exposed to a currency risk. It should wherever possible try to match currencies or foreign exposure immediately in the correct way, by using an appropriate foreign exchange hedging service or one of the other tactics described in this chapter.

In this chapter we have explained currency options and swaps that are examples of a derivative. There are others. A derivative is an instrument whose performance is based on the price variations of an underlying asset. For example, a currency option is based on the underlying foreign exchange market. In a derivative transaction the underlying asset does not need to be bought or sold. It requires no movement of principal funds at maturity. The detailed study of derivative markets is beyond the scope of this book. Recommended further reading for those interested is *Mastering Derivatives Markets* by Francesca Taylor.

CHAPTER ELEVEN

COMPANY TAXATION AND FINANCIAL MANAGEMENT

As non-finance managers, I thought it would be useful for you to know some of the elements of company taxation and how they affect financial decisions. This is quite a challenge for me since taxation is an enormous subject in its own right and each country has its own set of rules and regulations. I must, therefore qualify this chapter at the start as providing a basic understanding of how tax systems might operate and not as a practical guide that can be used to calculate your tax liabilities. Taxation affects all management decisions, and to leave this subject out would leave a gap in your understanding of the principles of corporate financial management.

I have worked in the UK and in New Zealand as a tax accountant and tax manager, and have a useful knowledge of Australian taxation as well as some limited knowledge of US taxation. I shall use this experience to explain how taxation principles can be brought into the financial management decision process.

The principal focus of this chapter will be on understanding the taxation implications of decisions and how to plan for these. It is possible, for example, that taxation will affect each project or business opportunity differently. It must, therefore, be considered. We are not interested in tax avoidance schemes, for which most regimes have set up extensive anti-avoidance regulations, or in tax evasion, which is of course illegal. Neither are we concerned with ways to minimize taxation. We are simply going to outline some basics that will help provide an understanding of the taxation implications of financial structures and decisions so that they can be properly considered and planned for.

Since this text does not restrict itself to financial management in any one taxation regime, I will provide generic examples of tax principles. Any rates quoted are simply hypothetical and not actual rates.

Direct and indirect taxation

Most countries differentiate between direct and indirect taxation and use a blend of both types. The principal classifications are outlined below.

Direct taxation

Direct taxes are those that are levied directly on earnings, profits or gains. They are charged on both companies and individuals. Examples of direct taxation are:

- corporation tax or company tax, UK;
- income taxes and National Insurance, UK;
- capital gains tax, UK;
- inheritance tax;
- business income tax, NZ;
- fringe benefit tax, NZ.

Indirect taxation

Indirect taxes are levied on expenditure. Examples of indirect taxes are:

- Value Added Tax (VAT) in the UK;
- Goods and Services Tax (GST) in Australia and in NZ;
- customs duties;
- purchase taxes;
- sales and excise taxes, US.

In addition to the above there is a whole raft of other taxes including:

- business rates, UK;
- property taxes, Au;
- petroleum revenue taxes;
- fuel taxes, Au;
- excise taxes, Au.

In some counties there can also be regional variations in tax rules.

Taxation authorities

The following are names of tax authorities that are mentioned in this chapter:

- HMRC: Her Majesty's Revenue & Customs, UK;
- IRD: The Inland Revenue Department, NZ;
- ATO: Australian Tax Office;
- CRA: Canadian Revenue Agency.

In the United States taxes are administered by very many tax authorities. At Federal level there are the three administrations of tobacco, alcohol and firearms taxes administered by the Alcohol and Tobacco Tax and Trade Bureau. Other domestic taxes are administered by the IRS (Internal Revenue Service). Import taxes are administered by the US Customs and Border Patrol. Each state has its own tax administration, and some states administer local taxes.

Your finance director or taxation manager will, of course, be your first contact on tax questions. If this is not possible, then it is often useful in the first instance to simply visit the website of the appropriate administration and search under the subject of your concern. The HMRC site in the UK is excellent. It provides online answers and also the contact numbers for each specialist area. Many topics are not so clear-cut, and you might then seek legal advice from a tax lawyer or the advice of a tax accountant.

Taxes on companies and corporations

Residence and the charge to corporation tax

Taxation on companies in the UK is referred to as corporation tax. In other regimes it may be referred to as business tax. For the purpose of this section I will make reference to the UK system of corporation tax since the principles are similar.

UK corporation tax is a tax that is charged on the global profits and chargeable gains of UK-resident companies. UK corporation tax is not charged on the dividends received from companies that are resident in the UK. A similar system applies in most other countries.

A company that is not resident in the UK but trades there through a branch or agency may also find that its profits are chargeable to UK corporation tax.

It is, therefore, important to understand all cross-border taxation implications of any overseas operations or plans.

Periods of assessment

Taxation periods of assessment may be different from accounting periods of assessment. This is an important consideration when planning tax liabilities, payments and cash-flow forecasts.

Where the taxation period is different from the financial accounting period it will be necessary to allocate profits between the periods, and it is always best to get agreement from HMRC to the method of allocation.

Tax laws, rates and treaties between countries are forever changing and since company residence, periods of assessment, rates and payments dates are critical to cash flow, it is important to plan taxation carefully before starting a new operation either domestically or overseas.

Basic calculation and payment of corporation tax

	£
Net profit per financial accounts after depreciation	3,000,000
Add back depreciation (not allowed)	30,000
Deduct capital allowances (tax depreciation)	−20,000
Profit chargeable to corporation tax	3,010,000
Corporation tax at say 30 per cent	903,000

The normal due date in the UK for the payment of corporation tax is nine months and one day after the end of the tax accounting period. However, in the case of companies that are designated as large (with profits of over £1.5m) corporation tax may be payable quarterly and, of course, there are special transitional rules for companies when they become designated as large.

Tax has to be paid on time to avoid penalties and interest. Interest will be charged on any overdue tax and this is not an allowable expense for taxation.

VAT and GST

Most countries have a form of indirect taxation that levies tax on goods and services when they are sold. For example, in the UK VAT is charged to buyers by VAT-registered sellers and in Australia there is GST (Goods and Services Tax), which is based on similar principles.

VAT is charged in the UK on business-to-business and business-to-end-consumer transactions and it may also be charged on goods and services imported from places outside the EU.

The tax is charged by a VAT-registered seller to a buyer. The VAT-registered seller is acting as a tax collector and will have to account to HMRC for the tax collected. If the buyer, who has paid the tax on goods purchased, is VAT registered, then s/he will call this input tax and will use it to offset or partially offset and output tax s/he has collected on services or products sold.

HMRC sets turnover limits for VAT registration. If a business exceeds this limit it must register for VAT. However, it may also register for VAT if it is below the limit. At the present time you may have to register if your sales are over £73,000 for the last 12 months; otherwise you may be able to register voluntarily.

Certain items are outside the scope of VAT and these are called exempt. Examples of these are education and training (if certain conditions are met), subscriptions to certain membership organizations, the provision of credit, insurance and certain fundraising events by registered charities. Always check with HMRC or your indirect taxation authority to determine if a product or service is exempt. Get it wrong and you could face a huge bill for uncollected tax.

The charge to VAT

VAT is charged on most goods and services that a VAT-registered business provides in the UK. It is also charged on goods and on some services that are imported from countries outside the European Union (EU), and brought into the UK from other EU countries. It is charged when a VAT-registered business sells to either another business or to a non-business customer.

When a VAT-registered business buys goods or services on which VAT has been charged, it can generally reclaim the VAT paid.

There are currently three rates of VAT, depending on the goods or services the business provides. The rates are:

- standard: 20 per cent;
- reduced: 5 per cent;
- zero: 0 per cent.

Some goods and services are exempt from VAT or outside the UK VAT system.

- The difference between exempt and zero-rated is that:
  - Zero-rated goods or services count as taxable supplies, but they don't add any VAT to a selling price because the VAT rate is 0 per cent.
  - Goods or services that are exempt don't have any VAT charge and they're not taxable supplies.

Generally a business can't register for VAT or reclaim the VAT on purchases if it sells *only* exempt goods or services. If it sells *some* exempt goods or services, it may not be able to reclaim the VAT on all of its purchases.

If a business buys and sells mainly zero-rated goods or services, it can apply to HMRC to be exempt from registering for VAT. This might be advantageous if it pays little or no VAT on purchases.

Indirect taxes and the economy

Indirect taxes such as VAT (UK) and GST (Au and NZ) are a simple and largely unavoidable way of collecting taxes. They are also less expensive to administer and provide a government with greater control over fiscal policy. Indirect tax rates can be changed quickly in response to economic events. They can quickly change spending patterns.

Some might argue that indirect taxes provide a better incentive in the labour market than direct taxes because they create less of a disincentive to work. This is because employees believe that they retain more of their earnings. There may be some truth in this because the argument states that workers respond better to lower marginal rates of direct income tax by working more hours thereby increasing production.

Basically indirect taxes can be extremely responsive to economic and environmental changes, enabling a government to control human activity more readily and easily than they can through direct taxation.

Taxes on the earnings of employees

Most countries have a system of collecting income tax from the earnings of employees directly from their employers. In the UK the system is called Pay As You Earn (PAYE).

The UK PAYE is the system that HM Revenue & Customs (HMRC) uses to collect Income Tax and National Insurance contributions (NICs) from employees' pay as they earn it. Employers have to deduct tax and NICs from their employees' pay for each pay period and pay Employer's Class 1 NICs if they earn above a certain threshold. These amounts are paid to HMRC monthly or quarterly. There may be penalties and interest charges for late payment. After the end of the tax year the company sends HMRC an Employer's Annual Return (forms P35 and P14). Most employers are now required to file this online.

Each employee is given a tax code by HMRC that will reflect their personal allowance and other adjustments. This code will be given to the employer and used in its payroll system to ensure that the correct amount of tax is deducted.

Global tax planning

Financial planners and accountants will need to understand the impact of different taxation regimes on the company's global operations. Global tax planners will need to understand different tax rules, the commercial validity of transactions, arm's length rules between related companies, double-taxation treaties, transfer pricing rules and many other aspects that can affect a strategic decision.

When considering the taxation implications of overseas activities and investments, the following require special attention:

- the definition of a resident – which varies from country to country;
- the fact that non-residents may be taxed in some countries;
- taxable income and allowable expenditure definitions – which vary between countries;
- variations in tax depreciation rules;
- definitions of a taxable person;
- different tax rates between countries;
- the timing of tax due dates;
- double tax treaties;
- definition of a permanent establishment;
- transfer pricing rules;
- arm's length rules;
- the commercial validity of transactions;
- tax avoidance definitions and tax avoidance provisions; consequences of avoidance;
- tax evasion and consequences;
- what is considered as acceptable taxation behaviour in different countries.

The above list is not exhaustive but highlights some of the areas that need to be considered if you are planning overseas activities.

The basic position in the UK is that any UK resident company that makes an overseas investment will be expected to pay UK taxes on income received before the deduction of foreign taxes. Any gain on sale of a foreign asset will also be taxed. This means that the starting point is that in addition to incurring UK tax on overseas activities there may also be foreign tax liabilities. However, double-taxation relief may be available. For this reason you will need to receive advice from experts or directly from HMRC and other taxation authorities to confirm the precise position.

Most taxation authorities do not like companies setting up name plates overseas to avoid taxation and controlled-foreign-company (CFC) and motive-testing rules exist to help prevent tax avoidance.

Double-taxation relief

Relief for double taxation may be available under reciprocal treaties with foreign countries. These allow for tax paid in one country to be deducted from a tax liability in another. Unilateral relief in relation to a particular tax where there is no treaty relief available may be given. If treaty or unilateral relief is not available then it might be possible to deduct overseas tax from overseas income before calculating local tax. Double-taxation relief is complex and advice should be taken from the taxation authorities or from a taxation practitioner.

Transfer pricing

World trade involves multinational enterprises (MNEs) and more than half of world trade is through associated party transactions. The price at which goods or services are transferred between one part of an organization and another is referred to as the transfer price. Transfer pricing is one of the most important issues MNEs face, and tax authorities around the world are updating their rules and regulations on international transactions as well as increasing their audit activity.

Since the behaviour of MNEs impacts significantly on tax collections, the community expects MNEs to contribute their fair share via the tax system, and transfer pricing is expected to have greater visibility and commercial justification. Identifying which pricing practices are legitimate can be a difficult task. Taxation authorities around the world have established departments to investigate transfer prices. Most countries will expect that a transfer price must be set at arm's length and reflect the market price at the time it was set.

Bringing taxation into the decision-making process

We have discussed in this chapter how taxation might affect the activities and cash flow of a company. Taxation must, therefore, be introduced into the decision-making processes.

Firstly, it must be recognized that every decision a company makes has a taxation implication and taxation will affect:

- costs;
- prices;
- cost of capital;
- cash flow;
- domicile;
- dividend policy;
- project costs;
- opportunity evaluation;
- all financial aspects and plans of an organization.

To evaluate alternative decisions, it is necessary to understand and bring into the equation the various taxation implications and options available. For example, this can be done by evaluating the present value of tax benefits associated with an investment and bringing these into an investment appraisal calculation.

Method of bringing tax benefits into account in an investment appraisal:

1 Calculate the present value of capital allowances (tax depreciation).

2 Multiply this by the tax rate.

3 This will give the present value of the tax benefit.

4 Deduct this present value of the tax benefit from the initial outlay on the project to give a net after-tax cost.

Taxation and the economy: future trends in tax collection

Annual income twenty pounds, annual expenditure nineteen pounds nineteen and six, result happiness. Annual income twenty pounds, annual expenditure twenty pounds ought and six, result misery.

(MR MICAWBER)

In this section we will take a look at tax collection, using the UK as an example.

In the year ended 2010 the UK government collected £409 billion in taxes. It collected this sum from the following sources:

Source of tax	£ billions
Income Tax	145
National Insurance Contributions	96
Value Added Tax	70
Corporation Tax	36
Fuel Duties	26
Tobacco	9
Spirit, Beer & Wine Duties	9
Stamp Duties	9
Air Passenger Duty	2
Capital Gains Tax	3
All other sources	4
Total	409

In addition, £21 billion of council tax was collected in England by local authorities and a little less than £2 billion in Scotland.

In 2010 in the UK the total central and local government spending was £689 billion. The major categories of spend were:

Expenditure	£ billions
Pensions	123
Health care/welfare	122
Education	84
Defence	46
Welfare	113
Protection	35
Transport	20
General government	24
Other	79
Interest	43
Total	689

Now, you don't need to be Mr Micawber to realize that the above figures will result in 'misery' unless the books are balanced. Of course, the UK government is working on this and you can draw your own conclusions. However, it is worth looking at more efficient and less expensive ways of collecting taxes.

The two simplest ways of collecting tax are through VAT and through a system of flat tax. Both of these systems reduce tax administration costs, are unavoidable and enable a government to make quick and easy adjustments to their tax take. We have already discussed VAT and the similar GST methods.

Flat tax is growing in popularity around the world, with currently around 30 countries either adopting or seriously considering it. A great advantage to taxpayers is that they no longer need to spend large amounts of time completing tax returns and claiming/justifying allowances. It also makes a whole raft of tax advice and administration unnecessary, freeing up people to undertake more valuable work. A true flat rate tax is when one tax rate is applied to all taxable income with no exceptions or exemptions. Of course, a change such as this would be highly contentious in a country such as the UK.

Probably the easiest way to make flat tax acceptable to most people would be to reduce the rates of income tax to a single rate and make up any shortfall with an increase in VAT. Looking at the above figures you can do the sums. However some people, including some economists, prefer the existing system. The debate will go on.

Summary

Taxation is a big-impact item. It has a huge effect on the bottom line and just about every decision a company makes. Yet, it is often forgotten or misunderstood by decision makers. It has been a challenge to decide what to cover in such a short space as this that will be of use to you as a manager or decision maker. Hopefully I have outlined some key areas and enabled you to present some appropriate questions to your financial director.

This chapter has been concerned with explaining the taxation implications of decisions so that they can be taken into account. It has not been concerned with aggressive tax minimization since this may be a high-risk strategy and one that is outside a company's core competence. Certainly there is always a cost for complexity and this should not be underestimated! Most companies want to be responsible citizens and value their relations with governments and taxation authorities.

CHAPTER TWELVE

THE VALUE OF A BUSINESS

Building value

There are many factors that affect the value of a business, some of which are more controllable than others. In broad terms businesses would expect to have an influence on most internal factors but little influence over external factors. Accordingly, a business that is highly sensitive to many external factors might find it more difficult to ensure a controlled increase in its valuation. Some of the principal internal and external factors that affect a business value are:

- Internal factors:
  - financial strength;
  - quality of executive team;
  - quality of staff;
  - quality of services and products;
  - resources;
  - agility and responsiveness;
  - customer perception and loyalty;
  - efficiency and profitability;
  - dividend policy;
  - building brand awareness.
- External factors:
  - the economy;
  - interest rates;
  - political and socio-economic environment;

- supply chain;
- labour supply;
- competition;
- industry;
- foreign exchange rates;
- environmental responsiveness.

Brand acceptance

A principal objective of most businesses is to increase their value. Value is sensitive to all of the above factors. Accordingly a business must identify which key internal factors it needs to excel in and how it can position itself in such a way as to minimize its exposure to the largely uncontrollable external factors. For example, developing a strong unique selling proposition (USP) might reduce a company's exposure to competition for a while.

A business should determine which factors affect its value the most, and have a plan and strategy to perform well in these. To do this it might carry out a strategic value analysis (SVA). This is a systematic measurement of each part of a business with a view to establishing how it might add value to the business. This will include an examination of core strengths and a comparison with external providers of services that might be outsourced.

Developing a target for a business valuation at a point in time in the future can help focus business strategy. For example, is there an intention to sell the business in the future, to float or go public, or is it preferred to keep the company under substantially the same ownership and control? Understanding how the business will be valued is also important. Understanding who you want to value the business and why they should value it is also a key consideration. A quoted company will be valued by the markets with particular attention to its price-earnings ratio. However, a company may have other value that is not so easily measured that could greatly affect its future earnings and valuation.

Business value is perhaps linked to the network of internal and external relationships. This is sometimes referred to as a value chain or value network where value is created as a result of collaboration between parts of the network. Company controls and processes are not the only things that create value. Understanding the value chain and relationships is key to value creation.

So far in this book we have discussed ways of measuring and improving performance. These are all essential to business success and value creation but so also are relationships and collaborative management of the value chain.

Methods of valuing a business

The economic value of a business is used by buyers and sellers to determine the price they are prepared to buy or sell a business for. It is necessary for all mergers and acquisitions. A business valuation is also used for estate, taxation and a number of other legal purposes.

Before a valuation can be undertaken it is necessary to understand the reasons for the valuation. For example, a valuation of a ship for scrap will be different from its valuation as a cargo carrier.

A value will take account of the price that a willing buyer and a willing seller will agree to. This is called the fair market value (FMV). The market conditions may, however, be far from perfect. For this reason a business valuation will usually start with a contextual evaluation of the economic and industry conditions surrounding the business. Is it a buoyant market or is it in recession? An analysis of the business's financial performance and strength will be compared to the rest of the industry. The valuations placed on competitors will be taken into account.

Common approaches to an initial business valuation are:

- income/earnings valuations as a going concern;
- asset valuations as a going concern;
- break up asset valuations;
- market valuations as a going concern.

Each of the above approaches will relate to a particular reason for selling or buying. Often a business will be valued on several bases and the differences between the valuations explained.

Before deciding upon which is the most appropriate valuation method the reason for a valuation will be considered. Possible reasons include:

- The valuation of a company to compare with the offer price of a takeover bid. These can also be compared with the current share price.

- A valuation may be required when a company goes into liquidation.
- A shareholder may require a valuation when wanting to dispose of a significant number of shares that might give a buyer a controlling interest.
- A valuation may be required for bankers when requesting new or additional finance.
- When going public an unquoted company may need a valuation to determine an issue price for its shares.
- Valuations are needed when companies merge.
- Valuations are needed for management buy-outs.
- Loan collateral may require periodic valuations.
- A taxation authority may require a valuation.

Some of the more common methods used for business valuations are outlined below.

The book value

This is based on the value of an owner's equity as recorded in the accounts. This may be a starting point but, unfortunately, accounting records may not reflect the true value of assets and liabilities. For example, the generally accepted accounting practice (GAAP) requires that stocks are valued at the lower end of cost or net realizable value. The good reason for this is conservatism. At the point of a business sale however, stocks may be worth a lot more or a lot less than the value recorded in the accounts. It all depends on what value the buyer can derive from the stocks. A buyer may have access to markets in which the stocks could be converted into cash at a higher price than is recorded in the accounts.

The tangible book value

This method simply values tangible assets and places no value on goodwill or other intangibles. Book values are adjusted by removing intangibles.

The economic book value

This method takes account of all assets including goodwill and values them at the market rate.

Net present value of future earnings

Future earnings are discounted, using an appropriate discount rate to give their net present value.

Income capitalization method

This method first of all establishes a capitalization rate, which is the rate of return required for the business risk. It then divides earnings by this rate.

Price earning multiple

This is the market price of a company's shares divided by its earnings per share multiplied by the net income.

Dividend capitalization

This is a company's dividend-paying capacity based upon its net income and cash flow.

Sales and profit valuations

Sales and profit multiples may be benchmarked in an industry and used for a valuation.

Realizable values

This method determines the net realizable value of assets on a company break-up assumption.

Replacement values

This method estimates the replacement value of a business. For example, how much would it cost a buyer to set up a similar business?

Who can value a business and what information do they require?

A business valuer will need to have a thorough understanding of the industry sector of the business and of each of the disciplines required in the valuation methods. For this reason it is likely to be an accountant, a lawyer or a senior banker who has been involved in the sector.

The information required will depend on the business and the importance of that information within the sector. Essential information will include:

- audited financial statements for most recent and past years;
- financial projections and the basis on which they are made;
- current sales orders and contracts;
- basis of cost estimates;
- supplier contracts and listings;
- aged debtors and creditors listings;
- cash-flow statements and forecasts;
- outstanding debts not yet invoiced, accruals, payments in advance, prepayments;
- basis of stock valuations for raw materials, work in progress and finished goods;
- stocktakes;
- assessment of stock obsolescence;
- property titles;
- land surveys;
- lease and rental agreements;
- loans schedules;
- schedules of investments and securities;
- bank statements and statements for all financial institutions;
- cash book;
- bank reconciliations;
- employment contracts;
- payroll;
- details of directors;
- directors and employee interests;
- organization chart;
- schedule of legal charges;
- debenture documents;
- industry and competitor information;
- list of shareholders, holdings and types of shares.

The precise information and depth of investigation required will depend upon the nature of the valuation and the type of business. The above list is not exhaustive. However, it will give you an idea of the potential areas that need to be covered when arriving at a valuation.

Examples of valuation methods and their appropriateness to valuation reasons

Here we will describe some of the valuation methods mentioned above in a little more detail and discuss how appropriate they are to different situations. Of course, real values are what is actually realized on sale. However, valuations are made without the benefit of a realized selling price and are at best just estimates.

Asset-based valuations

An asset-based valuation may provide a fundamental base and check that can be used to question the results from other valuation methods. They are sometimes referred to as floor values. However, asset-based valuations, just like other methods, need to consider the premise or reason for the valuation. For example, it is generally accepted accounting practice that stocks should be recorded in the accounts at the lower end of cost or net realizable value. However, in a business valuation should they be valued at replacement value, realizable value or scrap value? The answer will depend upon the intentions of the buyer of the business. Do they want to carry on as a going concern or is it their intention to drop the stock line and sell it off? Or will stocks just be scrapped? The value will depend upon what use the buyer can put them to.

Example

Fixed assets	€400,000,000
Depreciation	(€200,000,000)
Goodwill	€90,000,000
Current assets – stocks at lower end of cost or net realizable value	€30,000,000
Current assets debtors and cash at bank	€80,000,000
Current liabilities	(€100,000,000)
Total net assets	€300,000,000

Deduct goodwill included in the above	€90,000,000
Total tangible assets less current liabilities	€210,000,000
Term loans	(€130,000,000)
Net asset value	€80,000,000
Number of ordinary shares	2,000,000
Net asset value per share	€40

If we deduct the intangible asset of goodwill, the net asset value per share is €40. However, goodwill may indeed have a value to a particular buyer or group of buyers. The basis of goodwill valuation will need to be examined to understand its component parts. For example, how much of this goodwill relates to the brand being purchased? Does this have value to the buyer or will the buyer be dropping the brand for a more powerful one? How much of the goodwill relates to customers and suppliers and will this have value in the future?

Stocks have been valued in accordance with accounting conventions. However, what is their real value to this particular buyer or to the market the sale is aimed at? Will the stock simply be disposed of at a low price or does it have a higher realizable value to the new buyer?

Fixed assets are in the accounts at a net book value of €200m (€400m – €200m of depreciation). What is the realizable value of these assets, what is their value as a going concern, what income can they generate, what is the current replacement cost, what is their expected life and what real value are they to the buyer? It could be a different value from €200m.

At best an asset-based valuation provides a floor value. It can cause confusion if not analysed but if it is properly understood in relation to a buyer's needs it can provide a useful base upon which to consider the earnings-based valuations, which we will now consider.

Earnings-based valuations

An earnings or profits-based approach to business valuations enables buyers to understand their possible future return on their investment on the assumptions that the business is a going concern and will continue to make the profits recorded and forecast. These, of course, are two big assumptions in many cases and this is why asset-based valuations are also used to bring valuations back to a more fundamental view.

Two earnings-based valuations are the price–earnings method and the earnings–yield method.

The price–earnings ratio and business valuation

This method uses the following formulae:

$$Market\ value = Earnings\ per\ share \times Price\ Earning\ Ratio$$

or

$$MV = EPS \times P/E\ ratio$$

Where:

$$EPS = \frac{Profit\ attributable\ to\ ordinary\ shareholders}{Weighted\ average\ number\ of\ ordinary\ shares}$$

$$P/E\ Ratio = \frac{Market\ value}{Earnings\ per\ share}$$

The earnings–yield method

$$Earnings\text{-}yield = \frac{Earnings\ per\ share}{Market\ price\ per\ share} \times as\ \%$$

$$Market\ value = \frac{Earnings}{Earnings\ yield}$$

Cash-flow valuations

Dividend valuation model

$$Market\ value\ (ex\ div) = \frac{Annual\ dividend\ expected\ in\ perpetuity}{Shareholder's\ required\ rate\ of\ return}$$

There is an assumption in this method that an equilibrium price for a share on the market is the discounted expected future income stream.

The expected future annual income stream for a share is the expected future dividend in perpetuity. The equilibrium price is the present value of the future income stream.

Dividend growth model

$$Market\ value = \frac{\text{Expected dividend in one year's time}}{\text{Shareholder's required rate} - \text{growth rate}}$$

Example

The dividend paid by CM plc this year was €400,000. It is expected to grow by 4 per cent per annum. The company's shareholders expect and require a return of 10 per cent per annum. Calculate the value of CM plc using the dividend growth model.

$$MV = \frac{€400,000\ (1.04)}{0.10}$$

$$MV = €4,160,000$$

Discounted-cash-flow (DCF) method of valuation

This method simply discounts the expected future cash flow from an investment using the cost of capital after tax as a discount rate. For example, if an investor expects to receive returns of £30,000 per year at each of the years 0 to 2 and £40,000 at year 3, when it has a cost of capital after tax of 9 per cent during the entire period, then the value of the investment using the DCF method would be:

Year	Cash flow	9% discount factor	Present value (€)
0	€30,000	1.000	30,000
1	€30,000	0.917	27,510
2	€30,000	0.842	25,260
3	€40,000	0.772	30,880
		NPV	113,650

Using the discounted-cash-flow method of valuation, the investor would not want to pay more than €113,650 for CM plc.

The value to other investors would be different if they had a different cost of capital.

Summary

We have worked through some of the more popular methods of business valuation. There are other methods that are not so widely used, but those described above are the essential methods that you need to know. At this point, it would be a worthwhile exercise for you to go online and obtain the financial statements and prices for a well-known company and to prepare your own valuation using three methods:

- the asset-based valuation method;
- the earnings–yield method;
- the discounted-cash-flow method.

You can choose any company. For example go to **www.j-sainsbury.co.uk** and the landing page will show the share price. Then search under Annual Report to find Financial Statements and then Balance Sheet and other statements.

Compare the results using different valuations and consider how each valuation might relate to different types of buyer.

In the case of bigger listed companies there will be a wealth of market information and prices available to assist in a valuation. This will not be the case for smaller companies where the valuation methods will have less market data to use.

At times market sentiment may influence valuations far more than the underlying fundamentals. At times of recession values may become related to fundamental analysis. Most valuations will use a mixture of income, asset and market information.

CHAPTER THIRTEEN

FINANCIAL STRATEGY

Financial strategy underpins a company's mission and goals. It ensures financial resources are available to achieve the objectives laid out in a corporate strategy.

When an organization commits to a business strategy it will need the capital infrastructure in place to support it. It will also need to have enough financial resource availability to capitalize on future opportunities and to cover contingencies. In doing this it will also want to ensure that financial resources are the correct strategic mix and are deployed at the most efficient cost. A financial strategy should, therefore, seek to:

- provide the capital infrastructure to support organizational aspirations;
- provide financial agility;
- provide the lowest cost of finance;
- provide the correct mix of financial resources;
- cover financial risks.

With the correct financial structure in place an organization has a better chance of being able to take forward its strategic vision and to build a sustainable future.

A financial strategy may typically have the following components.

Financial environmental scan of the industry sector

This is an analysis of the demand for and availability of finance in the sector. What appetite do equity investors have to invest in the industry sector? How is it perceived in the financial markets? Is the rest of the sector 'hungry' for finance? The sector demand and supply for finance will take account of the current and future economic conditions and of the perceived sector risk.

Financial environment of the organization

Consider the financial strength of the organization including the past few years' audited results, management accounts and financial projections. What is the current cash position, what cash will be required in future years and where will it come from? What is the ideal gearing ratio? How does the financial environment within the organization fit within the broader financial environment of the industry sector? How will the markets and the banks respond to a request for additional funds? How well will the organization respond to the expectations of its financial providers?

Elements of a financial strategy

A financial strategy has key tasks that help underpin an organization's mission, strategic aims and objectives. These include:

1 The development of financial performance objectives that will:
   - deliver profits or operating surpluses;
   - provide cash when required while ensuring optimal cash balances are achieved;
   - maintain financial viability and agility;
   - set working capital targets;
   - set target balance sheet and financial ratios;
   - set financial objectives and key performance indicators;
   - establish financial stakeholder requirements and relationship management;
   - maintain routine cost and budgetary controls and variance reporting;
   - require a regular review of financial objectives in light of actual performance.

2 Maintenance of financial capacity to meet strategic objectives including:
   - ensuring the company has the right level of financial capacity for key resources;
   - management of financial investments, their proper availability and bank relationships.
3 Ensuring funds are available on time for specific capital investments.
4 Assessing the implications of strategic developments and the evaluation and management of risks. This includes:
   - the prioritization of strategic goals;
   - the identification and management of financial risks;
   - risk and sensitivity analysis;
   - providing financial capacity;
   - providing financial agility;
   - financial contingency planning;
   - investment appraisal standards;
   - determining the cost of capital;
   - identifying strategic alliances.
5 Ensuring that the financial strategy is fully integrated and supports every element of the corporate strategy. This includes:
   - ensuring that the financial strategy is accepted by the organization's executive team;
   - ensuring that budget holders accept and understand the financial strategy;
   - holding regular reviews of the financial strategy;
   - adopting and agreeing to a new financial strategy to changes in conditions and if circumstances require.

Strategic financial management

Strategic financial management is concerned with creating value through financial efficiency and providing a financial environment that supports the goals, ambitions, ethos and ethical values of a company. It is not something that can be done in isolation but is a part of the corporate planning and governance process.

Most companies will prepare a SWOT analysis as part of their strategic plan. If, for example, during this process they identified that a lack of agility was a weakness and that interest rate increases were a threat, they might develop the following two high-level strategic goals:

- increase strategic agility to take advantage of future opportunities;
- reduce financial risks.

To help achieve these goals the following financial strategy may be appropriate:

Financial strategy	Link with overall business strategy
To increase strategic agility: Open credit lines with banks	Increased agility and ability to respond to new opportunities
Build additional banking relationships	Improved ability to raise new funds at short notice
Tighten working capital management	Improved cash balances to meet urgent requirements
Reduce costs	Improved profitability and cash availability
Replace some fixed costs with variable ones	Ability to change suppliers and business direction more easily
To reduce financial risks: Take out forward contracts to cover FX risks	Reduced direct foreign exchange risk
Hedge against interest rate risks	Reduced financial risk of interest rate increases on borrowing
Consider a reduction in gearing	May reduce exposure to interest rate risks on borrowing
Consider investment strategy	Reduced exposure to reductions in interest rates on investments

The above financial strategies clearly support the overall business strategy, and the finance director would seek to obtain executive agreement to them. By supporting the organizational goals the financial strategy will help create value within the company.

This alignment of financial strategy with overall corporate strategy must be completed before any operational financial strategy is developed. Whilst sound financial management can create value in its own right it must always be in alignment with overall business strategy. For example, reducing the cost of borrowing by placing facilities with one financial institution might also reduce a company's financial agility, and this might be in conflict with business strategy.

Financial strategy statements are sometimes included in reports to shareholders and members. They vary enormously depending upon the type of organization they relate to. An example of a simple financial strategy statement produced by a small town council is given below. You can see that it has addressed at least some of the elements we have discussed above:

Example of a financial strategy set out by a council

1 The main purpose of this finance strategy is to ensure that there are financial resources to support the strategic objectives of the Council. It should also support the supporting activities needed to achieve the strategic objectives.

2 This strategy sets out how to secure efficient financial resources needed to support the strategic objectives above, to ensure the long-term viability of the Council and to manage financial risks.

3 The finance strategy guides the Board to ensure that sound financial controls exist to protect the security of the Council's assets.

4 The strategic plan aims to provide those services set out in the Council's annual statement. The financial strategy supports this aim.

5 The systems that contribute to the achievement of the financial strategy are:
   – financial controls;
   – financial regulatory environment;
   – cash and reserves policy;
   – treasury management policy;

- investment policy;
- internal and external audit programmes;
- fixed asset register;
- purchasing controls and regulations;
- budgetary procedures;
- risk management and contingency plans;
- Board's code of practice;
- audit committee;
- systems development and protection.

6 What does financial success look like?
- Members and the public have confidence in the financial management of the Council.
- The Council has funds to implement its strategic objectives.
- Members have a clear view of the cost of activities and services.
- All expenditure is related back to a Council meeting minute giving approval.
- There are clear internal and external audits.
- Final accounts are filed on time.
- All taxes are paid on time.
- Budget holders understand their responsibilities.
- The Council's budget/precept is submitted on time.
- Financial risks are identified and covered.
- Funds are invested in accordance with the Council's policy in agreement with Borough and County Council guidelines.

7 Financial goals:
- to provide appropriate financial support to the Council's objectives set out in the strategy document;
- ensure that funds are collected on time;
- maintain banking relationships;
- meet statutory obligations;
- maintain rigorous financial controls.

8 Responsibilities for the finance strategy
- The finance committee is responsible for ensuring corporate governance, overall internal controls and risk management.
- The Audit Committee will report to Members on the effectiveness of internal controls, risk management, external and internal audit matters.

- Day-to-day responsibility for financial management is delegated by the Members to the Chief Executive and Finance Officer.
- Committee heads have responsibility as budget holders.
- The Finance Department will ensure that procedures are in place to comply with all the financial and statutory regulations.
- The Finance Director has overall responsibility for the Finance function and the development and implementation of the financial strategy.

As you would expect from a council handling public money, the emphasis is on risk control, accountability and strict investment guidelines. Even so, this did not prevent many county councils investing money with an Icelandic bank after its credit rating fell and eventually being unable to get their investments back. More about this subject in the chapter on case studies.

Integration of financial management with corporate strategy

The way that aspects of financial management integrate with corporate strategy can be seen in the summary below:

- **Value creation:**
  - identify value creating activities;
  - identify critical success factors;
  - identify drivers for change;
  - identify investment opportunities;
  - identify restructuring opportunities;
  - link to business goals.
- **Financial evaluation and analysis:**
  - evaluate financial implications of change;
  - link strategy to planning, budgeting and programming;
  - define strategic business units and measure their performance;
  - ensure that resources are justified from a zero base and are aligned to business goals;
  - identify the drivers of cost;
  - use management accounting techniques to measure performance and evaluate options;

- use a financial performance 'dashboard';
- identify opportunities for cost reduction.
- **Investment analysis and decision making:**
  - decide on an appropriate cost of capital for use in investment appraisals;
  - evaluate and prioritize investment opportunities;
  - use payback, DCF, NPV, IRR, cost–benefit and other evaluation techniques;
  - identify links between investment opportunities and current investments;
  - define and evaluate critical interdependencies;
  - prepare sensitivity analysis;
  - make decisions.
- **Mergers, acquisitions, MBOs and other restructuring opportunities:**
  - determine whether M&A opportunities fit with organizational strategic objectives;
  - establish value measurement for M&A;
  - determine the effect that a merger/acquisition will have on funding and the cost of funds;
  - evaluate the target's and merged cost structures after an acquisition;
  - identify risks;
  - evaluate M&A opportunities;
  - prepare risk and sensitivity analysis.

The above is not an exhaustive list but shows how financial management supports value creation.

Strategic change programmes

When considering strategic change programmes it is helpful to classify them into categories. For example the change may be due to *transition* (as may be required following a merger), *transformation* (changing products and processes) or *continuous* and ongoing improvements. The value of the change can be estimated by determining the benefits and costs:

TABLE 13.1 Benefits and costs of change

Nature of change	Potential financial benefits	Possible additional costs
Product streamlining	Reduced product costs Higher margins Higher sales volumes	Additional marketing Design, development, testing
Product development	Higher margins	Increased product costs Additional marketing
Process re-engineering	Lower processing costs	Consulting, implementation
Organizational streamlining	Reduced staffing costs Improved margins Increased efficiency	Redundancy pay outs Consulting
Quality improvement	Reduced costs Customer retention Additional customers Higher margins	Cost of change and consulting
Out-sourcing	Reduced costs Better organizational focus	Consulting Transition costs
Staff development	Fewer errors Staff retention Focus and productivity	Training costs Possible higher staff turnover
Mergers and acquisitions	More sales Better margins Additional opportunities	Advisors' fees Transitional costs

This table will be helpful when attempting to assess the key financial benefits to strategic change programmes suggested by your executive team. Some benefits and costs are easily identified; others are less tangible. The above list is not exhaustive and is only a first guide. For example, improved quality should reduce costs by reducing production interruptions; this is easily measured. It might improve customer retention and win additional customers, but this is not so easily estimated before the change.

Summary

As a manager your main task at all times is ensuring that you create value. You will need to know where value comes from and understand how it is built or eroded. This requires a strategic understanding of financial management and the ability to evaluate the financial consequences of your decisions.

Integrating finance and corporate strategy will help you and your finance director understand how you both contribute to value creation.

The following list has been prepared by researching best-practice financial strategy outlined in the professional syllabuses of a number of leading global accountancy institutions. It provides a good final summary of the actions that need to be taken to provide a sound financial strategy.

- Evaluate organizational objectives in financial terms.
- Determine strategic financial objectives.
- Evaluate the achievement of financial objectives.
- Determine the relationships between investment decisions, financing and dividend policy.
- Determine the impact of internal and external constraints on financial strategy including regulatory constraints.
- Evaluate business performance forecasts and risks, and prepare a sensitivity analysis.
- Determine and evaluate alternative financial strategies.
- Establish the short- and long-term financing requirements.
- Consider all financing and funding alternatives.
- Determine the most suitable method for calculating the organization's cost of capital.

- Calculate interest rate and currency exposure, and determine a hedging policy.
- Prepare a working capital management strategy.
- Establish the roles and parameters of the treasury function.
- Analyse the costs and benefits of investment opportunities.
- Make investment decisions that maximize financial objectives subject to capital rationing.
- Evaluate mergers, acquisitions, de-mergers and divestments.

CHAPTER FOURTEEN

THE COST OF CAPITAL

The cost of capital is the cost of funds used by an organization. It is the return that an organization gives to its providers of funds and reflects the perceived risk of providing those funds. An organization's capital comes from a variety of sources that have different rights to returns and security. Accordingly each element that makes up the cost of capital carries a different risk and, therefore, has a different cost. We need to consider how these components combine to make up an organization's cost of capital. It is an important element in decision making because the cost of capital can be used as a discount rate in investment appraisal calculations.

This chapter will help you choose an appropriate discount rate to use for investment appraisal using discounted-cash-flow and net-present-value techniques. This can be a subject that occupies the time of academics who spend a lifetime debating and arguing about the pros and cons of each method. Certainly it is an important subject, particularly for very large organizations making decisions that involve billions. However, I shall try to keep this discussion at a practical level and explain what I think will be useful to a practising business manager.

First of all we will discuss the two concepts of the average cost of capital and the marginal cost of capital.

The weighted average cost of capital (WACC)

A company has the following sources of capital:

Ordinary shares	€300K @ 10 per cent per annum
Long-term loans	€150K @ 6 per cent per annum
Short-term loans	€100K @ 8 per cent per annum
Total	€550K

Its weighted average cost of capital is:

$$\frac{(300 \times 10) + (150 \times 6) + (100 \times 8)}{550}$$

WACC = **8.55 per cent per annum**

The marginal cost of capital

If we assume that this company wishes to borrow more money but that the only funds currently available in the market for this level of risk are priced at 12 per cent per annum, then the marginal cost of capital is *12 per cent per annum.*

If additional capital is taken up at this marginal cost, then the weighted average cost of capital will increase.

The cost of ordinary share capital

We talked above about the costs of share capital and loan capital. Whilst it is easy to determine the cost of loan capital (the agreed rate in the contract) what is the actual cost of share capital or equity?

Whilst the directors are under no obligation to make regular dividend payments to ordinary shareholders it must be remembered that these shareholders generally carry the highest risk, own the company and quite rightly expect the highest return. Shareholders will also want to see the market value of their investment maintained or increased. Therefore, the cost of equity is the rate that needs to be paid to maintain shareholder value and to meet their expectations.

Example

A company earns 10p (after interest) per share and pays a regular dividend of 5p per share. The other 5p is kept in the business to help reduce gearing and will earn 5 per cent per annum. The current market value of a share is €1.70.

$$\text{The cost of equity capital} = \frac{\text{Dividend}}{\text{Market value}} \times 100 + \text{growth}$$

$$\text{or} \qquad E = \frac{d}{m} \times 100 + g$$

$$E = \frac{5p}{170p} \times 100 + 5\%$$

$$E = 7.94\%$$

The cost of equity capital is 7.94 per cent.

I have kept this simple to illustrate the basic calculation. However, in reality there are other costs associated with raising equity capital. A share issue will require advertising, underwriting, financial and legal advice and other costs. These costs can be estimated and will increase the cost of equity.

Balancing equity and external borrowing

When finding the optimal level of financial gearing, a company will wish to maximize the return on shareholders' funds whilst ensuring the financial stability of the company.

As we have discussed in previous chapters, when profits are high a highly geared company may be able to provide a greater return to fewer shareholders. However, when profits are low there might not be much left to distribute to shareholders after paying interest to external providers of finance. A highly geared company may be considered a greater financial risk by both external and new investors, raising the cost of capital. On the other hand, equity shareholders carry the greatest risk and will expect the greatest return, which might increase the cost of capital in a low-geared company.

The cost of capital may therefore relate to the cost of funds that a company uses, bearing in mind the return that investors expect and require. It is the minimum return that a company needs to make in order to pay investors their expected returns. It has been described as the opportunity cost of finance, since it is the minimum that investors require for the level of risk they are accepting. If investors do not get this required return they will put their funds elsewhere.

Risk and the cost of capital

The cost of capital will increase as perceived risk increases.

Risk-free rate of return

If there is no risk on an investment, as is the case with government securities for example, then the rate of return will be the lowest in the market. This is the risk-free rate.

The premium for a business risk

All businesses carry the risk of failure, of lower than expected results. There is always uncertainty surrounding business results. Accordingly an investor will require a premium over and above the risk-free rate for making a business investment. This is called the premium for business risk, and it will vary between businesses.

The premium for financial risk

Some companies carry a higher level of financial risk. For example a highly geared company may be more exposed to interest rate increases. Investors will require a higher premium for a higher financial risk.

Elements of the cost of capital

Cost of capital = Risk free rate + Premium for business risk
                               + Premium for financial risk

Different companies have different capital structures and varying costs of capital.

Dividend growth model

If we assume that the market value of a share is related to the expected future dividends from the shares, then the cost of providing required dividend growth can be used as a cost of capital. The method used to calculate the cost of equity taking this into account is the 'dividend growth model'.

However, there is a risk in holding shares in a specific company (unsystematic risk) and a further general market risk (systematic risk). An investor may seek to reduce systematic risk through diversification. However, specific unsystematic risk cannot be reduced in this way. The 'capital-asset-pricing model' is a method that can be used to calculate a cost of equity and incorporate risk.

Capital-asset-pricing model (CAPM)

This pricing model is used to determine the theoretical price of a security.

The expected return for a security is:

$$E_s = R_f + \beta_s(R_m - R_f)$$

where:

E_s = the expected return for a security
R_f = the expected risk-free return in the market (for example UK government bonds)
β_s = the sensitivity to market risk for the security
R_m = the historical rate of return on the stock market
$(R_m - R_f)$ = the risk-free premium of market assets over risk-free assets

Example

If the risk-free rate of return is 4 per cent when the average market return is 6 per cent and the sensitivity to market risk is 0.9, what is the expected return from a share?

Expected return = 4 per cent + 0.9 (6 per cent – 4 per cent)
Expected return = 5.8 per cent

Both the dividend-growth model and the CAPM methods have their advantages and disadvantages, and the finance director will calculate the cost of equity and the overall cost of capital using several methods before deciding which method is appropriate. Generally, these types of debate are more significant to a large company.

Summary

The cost of capital is the rate of return that a company has to pay to gain and retain funds from investors, who will take into account their risk in investing. It is the opportunity cost of investment capital or the marginal rate of return required by investors. When calculating a weighted average cost of capital in a low-geared company, the rate for the cost of equity that is included in the calculation might not be a factor to which the overall rate is particularly sensitive. You need to decide how sensitive investment appraisals are in your own organization to estimate a precise and academically sound cost of capital.

There are arguments for and against each method of calculating the cost of capital. This chapter has discussed some of the principal methods and explained the elements that make up the cost of equity and the cost of capital, and it is hoped that you can now decide which method is relevant to your own organization. In a large multinational organization an understanding of the true cost of capital may be considered to be important, whilst in a small company it might not be considered to be particularly material to most decisions.

CHAPTER FIFTEEN

DIVIDEND POLICY

When a company finds that it has more cash than it can retain in the businesses to provide an attractive return it may decide to pay the shareholders a dividend. If a business is retaining cash in the business that is not increasing the value of the business ahead of other investment opportunities for shareholders, then the shareholders can reasonably expect the company to pay out a dividend. It is the directors who decide on the size of dividends, and although shareholders might have the power to reduce a dividend they generally do not have the power to increase it. The directors decide on dividend policy.

The questions facing directors regarding dividend payments are around how much cash should be paid to shareholders and how much should be retained in the business for investment and for managing future market conditions and risks? When the directors have decided how much to pay to shareholders, the next question is what form the return should take.

Paying a dividend or keeping the funds in the company?

It would be very hard for a company to always find new investment opportunities for the surpluses and retained funds generated by its operations. In most cases a successful and profitable company will find that it needs to pay a dividend since this is the best option for shareholders. It may be impossible for a company to profitably re-invest every pound it makes. When a company pays dividends this should not be construed by the markets as meaning that the company is running out of new ideas, since in most cases having funds available is inevitable with successful companies. New opportunities in a sector may not keep pace with earnings generated.

What form should a distribution take?

A company may wish to pay a consistent and predictable dividend. If a company cannot be sure of a consistent dividend level it might consider alternatives such as buying back shares. A share re-purchase has the advantage that it gives the shareholder the choice of whether or not to participate.

Influences in dividend policy

The following are some of the main questions that influence a company's dividend policy:

- How much of the existing retained earnings need to be retained for future financing needs (both operational and in terms of new investment opportunities)?
- What new investment opportunities exist?
- What are current interest rates?
- What other investment opportunities exist for shareholders at this time?
- Will the company remain profitable?
- Is the proposed distribution legal? For example, in the UK dividends can only be paid out of accumulated net realized profits.
- Do any loan agreements restrict the size of dividend payments?
- Does the company have enough cash to pay dividends?
- Are there any existing government constraints on dividend payments?
- How much profit should be retained in the business to maintain existing operations?
- Are any loans due for repayment? Will enough profits be retained to make these loan repayments?
- What will a distribution indicate to the markets? Will it be received favourably or will it be perceived as a sign that the company has run out of new ideas?

- How will this distribution affect the company's gearing target?
- How easy will it be in the future to raise extra finance?

Dividend policy determination is very much a strategic decision. Financial efficiency is only a part of the decision, which should also consider signals to investors, future market trends, the ability to invest profitably in new opportunities and the company's future financial needs.

Dividend policy theories

From the above influences on dividend payment levels have arisen a number of theories regarding dividend payments that might help to classify them into different categories.

The residual theory

This theory states that only when a company can no longer identify any investment opportunities with a positive net present value should it pay a dividend. In other words, a company should not pay dividends if it can positively identify investments in new projects with a positive NPV.

The traditional view

This theory assumes that a market share price depends upon the mix of dividends expected by shareholders, and that dividend policy should reflect this.

The irrelevancy theory

This theory concludes that the value of a company is based upon the earning power of its assets and investments and that, in a tax-free world, a company's shareholders have no preference between dividends and capital gains. Accordingly, dividend policy is irrelevant. This theory was the view of Modigliani and Miller. There are arguments for and against this theory and, rather than list these here I will let you form your own opinion, which I am sure is as good as any others. The Modigliani and Miller theory is well referenced on the web if you have an academic interest in their work.

The optimal dividend policy theory

This theory argues that there exists an optimal dividend policy that will strike a balance between dividend payments and growth that will maximize a company's share price on the market.

The dividend relevancy theory

This theory assumes that the value of a company is affected by dividend policy and that an optimal dividend policy may be reached that will maximize a company's value.

There is much debate regarding the effect of dividend policy on share valuation, and for the purpose of this text it is sufficient for you to be aware of the various theories.

Ways of paying dividends

When a company has decided to pay a dividend the next decision is how to pay it. Should it be by cash, a scrip issue, stock split or by a share repurchase? I will describe these below.

Cash dividend

If the company has accumulated surplus funds and can retain adequate levels of funding for its future needs together with adequate cash lines in place, it might want to consider paying a cash dividend.

Scrip dividends

This is a dividend paid by the issue of additional shares. This retains cash in the company. In certain circumstances the directors will offer shareholders the choice between a cash dividend or a scrip dividend. Sometimes the scrip dividends will be offered at a greater value that the cash dividend option.

The advantages of a scrip dividend to the company are that cash is retained and that the issue will decrease the level of gearing, which may have a positive effect on its borrowing capacity. A disadvantage is that the issue might dilute the share price, although a small scrip issue may have no significant effect.

From the investors' point of view there may be tax advantages in receiving their dividend in the form of shares, and they can also increase their holding without having to pay the costs involved in purchasing additional shares.

Stock split

A stock split leaves reserves in place and simply splits the existing shares into smaller denominations. For example, existing €2 shares may be split into shares of €1 each. This may improve the market trading in the shares and push up their price. As an example, a €2 share may be traded on the market at €2.20 whereas, when split into €1 shares, the new €1 denominations may trade at €1.15 thus giving existing holders a market valuation gain of 10p over their original value (2 × €1.15 – €2.20). There is, of course, no logical reason why this should be the case, but perhaps investors just like trading in smaller denominations, lose track or just assume that because the shares have been split the company has growth plans. Whatever the underlying reasons, a split may have a positive effect on market prices and increase existing shareholders' valuations, or returns if they sell.

Share repurchase

A company must check whether it is 'legal' to purchase its own shares according to the laws in place in its country. In many countries, subject to certain conditions, companies do have the right to buy back shares from shareholders who want to sell.

Some large companies buy back their own shares in order to pull out of the listed share market and go private. The benefits of a share repurchase include using up surplus cash that is not generating value, increasing gearing (when this may be seen as beneficial) and increasing the earnings per share. Disadvantages are that a shareholder may suffer tax disadvantages (capital gains tax v other taxes) and that it might be difficult to determine a price. However, these aspects will be considered by shareholders who can make their own decision as to whether to sell.

Summary

A company's dividend policy has a significant impact on its financial health. For example it affects liquidity, the cost of capital, the market value of shares and the market perception of a company. Some companies that can guarantee high returns on their capital have a zero dividend policy, providing value to shareholders through the increased market value of their shares.

It is a potentially very complex subject in a large multinational company with overseas subsidiaries, associates and investments.

This short chapter has outlined some of the more important factors that you might want to be aware of. The main things to remember are that retained earnings are the most important source of finance for most companies. Generally, dividend payments are smoothed out to avoid large fluctuations that might alarm investors and reduce their confidence.

CHAPTER SIXTEEN

CASE STUDIES

In the previous chapters we have covered some of the basic principles that need to be applied for sound corporate and business financial management. It will be beneficial to see how some of the more important principles work in practice, and so this chapter provides real case studies that demonstrate good and bad practice. For the purpose of confidentiality I have not named any companies or banks.

In recent years the banks have come under considerable criticism, most of which they deserve. You will see examples in these cases. However, you will also see cases of poor financial management by corporates, and I am sure that you can add to this list.

It is hoped that these cases will help you recognize both good and bad financial management behaviour within your own organizations.

Case 1.   Misuse of short-term funds with disastrous consequences.

Case 2.   Foreign exchange hedging v speculation.

Case 3.   Stock valuations and profits.

Case 4.   Bank loans and covenants.

Case 5.   Separating money transmission from a lending bank.

Case 6.   Credit ratings and fundamental analysis.

Case 7.   Advantages and disadvantages of internal charging.

Case 8.   Marginal costing v fully integrated standard costing.

Case 9.   Overtrading: profits but no cash.

Case 10.   Integrating the planning and budgeting process, leading to outsourcing.

Case 11.   Government deficits and cost cutting.

Case 12.   A 5 per cent increase in sales is generally worth more than a 5 per cent reduction in costs.

Case 13.   Large capital projects and cost control: critical path analysis and integration with mainstream accounts.

Case 14.   A mass of figures just makes life more complicated.

Case 15.   High levels of fixed costs when income is variable can cause failure.

Case 16.   Interest rates and inflation.

Case 1: Misuse of short-term funds with disastrous consequences

This was one of the saddest and most unnecessary closures of an excellent business by a bank that pulled the rug when its customer incorrectly used short-term funds (an overdraft) for long-term needs (purchase of a new freehold branch). I hasten to say that this was not one of my customers or a customer of my bank.

The business had been trading in the UK for more than 40 years under the same experienced proprietor. It had five branches, three of which were freehold and owned without a mortgage. The business had no significant borrowing but did have a €250k overdraft facility that it used from time to time to help ride the seasonality of its business.

An opportunity arose to purchase a new freehold branch for €400K and the proprietor wanted to grab what he considered to be a bargain. To do this he used surplus cash in the business and in addition unwisely used most of his overdraft facility to make up the balance. I say unwisely because, as we have discussed, an overdraft is short-term money that is repayable on demand. It should not be used for long-term needs such as the purchase of a new branch. Appropriate funding would have been a term loan but the proprietor did not apply for one, assuming that he could sort things out later with the bank if need be. He thought he had a good banking relationship.

Shortly after the new branch purchase, things started to go wrong for the company. A recession had brought about a sharp decline in trade and sales took a steep dive. A lot of the company's costs were fixed and it found itself in need of cash. It had already used up its own cash reserves and its overdraft facility.

The proprietor went to see his bank manager to ask for an increase in overdraft. This was a new manager with whom he had no relationship and who had little knowledge of his customer's business. He took the immediate view that he would not increase the overdraft limit since sales were in decline. He also explained that he would review existing limits in light of current business performance. His decision was that the limit would be reduced to €100k and that the business must achieve this immediately. This overdraft was repayable on demand.

As the company was unable to repay this amount the receivers were called in. The business was wound up and property was sold at the very low prices obtainable during a recession. The bank came away with its overdraft and the penalty charges it had loaded on. The proprietor came away with something but this was a fraction of what the business and property would have been valued at only a short time before. The saddest thing, though, was that a good business closed down leaving many people without work.

The important message here is that a business should not use short-term funds for long-term needs. Another message is that you can expect a bank to protect its own position first. It is not a benevolent organization. A bank relationships can be hard to maintain and not always worth a lot when you do. Keep your elbow room or you might find that you have to dispose of assets when the market for them is low.

Case 2: Foreign exchange hedging v speculation

This case involved a medium/large New Zealand company that needed to purchase US$30 million of technical equipment from the United States. At the time of capital budget sanction the rate of exchange was US$1=NZ$1.28. On the actual date of purchase the rate was US$1=NZ$1.37. The return on this investment by the New Zealand company was positive NZ$ and was based upon the rate of exchange at the time of budget sanction as follows:

Capital budget approved (US$30m @ 1.28)	NZ$38.4m
Income	NZ$40.4m
Return	NZ$2.00m (5.2 per cent)

(For the purpose of this illustration we will ignore the time value of money and discounted cash flow.)

To secure the return required at the time of budget sanction the NZ company needed to firm up (fix) the rate of exchange at US$1=NZ$1.28. Failure to do this might result in a loss on exchange that could partially (or more than) offset the expected return on the investment. In fact, failure to hedge against the exposure at the time of signing the contract for the equipment would leave the New Zealand company with an unlimited downside risk.

Since the company was cash rich, it decided to purchase the US$ at the time of budget sanction. Dealing lines were arranged and the US$ were purchased at a rate of US$1=NZ$1.28. The company would earn US$ interest on the funds purchased and forgo NZ$ interest on the NZ$ used to purchase the US$. At the time NZ and US interest rates were similar, and since the time between budgetary sanction and equipment purchase was only a few weeks, it was considered that any loss/gain on exchange on the interest differential was small compared with the avoidance of a loss/gain on the principal sum.

By taking this type of hedging action the company avoided (on this occasion) the following NZ$ loss:

Actual cost of US$30m @ 1.28	NZ$38.40m
Cost on equipment purchase date, US$30m @ 1.37	NZ$41.10m
Avoided loss	NZ$2.70m

Had the company not purchased the currency in advance, the loss on exchange would have more than offset the budgeted profit on the investment. The directors were satisfied that they had made the correct decision by protecting the return on their investment.

The following year the company needed to make another purchase of equipment from the United States for a similar amount. It followed the same process and purchased the US$ in advance. On this occasion the US$ v NZ$ rate of exchange moved in the opposite direction, and had the company not purchased the currency in advance then it would have made a gain on exchange on the day of equipment purchase. However, this would have been an unauthorized gain since the directors did not have the authority to speculate on the exchange markets. They would have received no thanks from the shareholders had they made a loss.

There were other alternatives to purchasing the currency in advance. The company could have taken out a forward contract and it might also have considered an option. An option contract would have limited the company's down side but not limited its potential gains. However, there is an argument that the part of an option price relating to the unlimited upside is a speculative investment and the directors would need to ensure that they had authorization to enter into such a contract.

The important point to understand here is that when a mismatch of currency results in an exposure, the duty of most finance directors is to eliminate or hedge against the exposure. They are not authorized to speculate unless that is the business of their organization.

Case 3: Stock valuations and profits

A small manufacturing company with 200 employees operated a fully integrated standard costing system.

Items manufactured used materials, labour and absorbed overheads as they travelled through the production process from raw materials to work in progress and finally finished stock. The system provided standards for material prices, materials used, labour rates and times, and overhead absorption rates. Standard rates were used to value stocks with some adjustment for variances.

At the year end a physical stock count would be taken and this usually produced a different result from the book stock recorded in the stock records and in the accounts. There were many reasons for this, including errors in the physical count, record-keeping errors, wastage, bookkeeping errors and a variety of clerical errors that occurred when recording thousands of transactions.

Now, the problem arose as to which valuation to use in the year-end accounts. Any difference between the stock value used and that currently recorded in the financial accounts would have a direct impact on the bottom line result.

Generally accepted accounting practice requires that stocks should be valued at the lower end of cost or net realizable value. However, which cost should be used, the actual cost of each item in stock or the standard cost? Most auditors would like to see stocks valued at their actual cost rather than standard costs, and they may look at the variances recorded by the standard costing system and apportion some of these variances back to the stock value rather than write the whole variance off into the profit-and-loss account. Then the question of which quantities are correct arises. Is it the physical count or the recoded quantities/values? It is too late to re-check the physical count after the stock-count day has passed because stocks would have moved since then. Generally auditors will prefer the physical count as long as it is performed properly, and this is why they should always be in attendance and check major value items themselves.

The company regularly changed its internal accountants and stock controllers. The auditors sought to ensure that there was consistency in the approach to valuation because any change in method would affect profits.

You can begin to see that amongst all these systems and processes that there was plenty of scope for error and inconsistency. The directors would read monthly management reports indicating profit levels based upon the results of the fully integrated standard costing system, and get a shock at the year end when the results had to be changed as a result of the physical stock take and the auditor's requirements.

Much time was spent trying to reconcile physical stock with book stock valuations, but generally little was achieved by these reconciliations.

The principal points to be aware of here are:

- Year-end physical stock valuations can have a dramatic effect on profits.
- There must be regular physical checks and reconciliations on book stocks and their values when a fully integrated standard costing system is used.
- Stocks should be valued at the lower end of cost or net realizable value.
- The actual cost of stock can be different from its standard cost, and it may be necessary to make adjustments to the stock values by considering variances.
- Consistency in valuation method is all important. The effect of any change in method should be separately reported.
- Stock obsolescence, wastage and loss will be discovered through the physical stock count and the examination of stock records.

Case 4: Bank loans and covenants

I came across this appalling case of bank mismanagement and customer naivety whilst visiting the business banking arm of a major bank operating in London. It is the sort of thing that makes banks unpopular and was in my mind entirely unnecessary. There is an argument that the bank's customer was at fault here and, technically, he was. However, I think the bank's action, whilst protecting its interest, was avoidable.

A small family-run business operated a successful camp site. It had plenty of spare land and decided that it would use this land to build cabins. The proprietor went to the bank to negotiate a loan to cover the building cost. A loan was offered for 60 per cent of the costs, with a first charge over the land and all buildings completed or partially completed and all materials on site. The bank also required the borrower to agree to certain covenants, which the borrower readily did, perhaps not realizing the significance of these. The covenants were many and varied, including things that the borrower must not do and things that he must do.

Among the things that the covenant required were to submit regular financial statements to the bank and to also maintain certain financial ratios, including liquidity and profitability. These must all have seemed easy enough to fulfil at the time.

Building works commenced in February and the proprietor expected to have at least five cabins completed by June and have them occupied by the time the school holidays commenced. This would have produced valuable income to assist with the rest of the building programme. Unfortunately, the builders (as is often the case) encountered delays in getting materials delivered and were hit by heavy rain that caused the whole programme to slip significantly. They would have several cabins completed by the school holidays, but what with other completions and ground work the site would not be suitable for residents. Then followed one of the wettest summers on record and people were just not camping. This meant that regular income from the site was down and that the business was running out of cash, with a delayed project and little chance of breaking even before the end of the season. This, you might think, must surely have been expected in such a seasonal business as camping. Why did the proprietor not allow for this and why did the bank not also factor it into their decision?

Of course, you can guess by now that when the borrower sent in the accounts to the bank, they did not show the required performance and he was in breach of covenant. The bank had headroom in its security and might have considered allowing the borrower a season to get things right. Perhaps it could have re-negotiated the loan and covenants. However, it was easier for the bank to simply pull the rug, load on penalty charges and clear its position.

So, what are the lessons learned here?

- Don't enter into any covenant lightly.
- Don't think you might not have to meet the terms of a covenant.
- Assume the bank will enforce the covenant.
- Understand the margin (the difference between its cost of borrowing and what it charges you) is often small in relation to the risk it is taking and that it will protect itself.
- A bank's principal responsibility is to its shareholders.

Case 5: Separating money transmission from a lending bank

Some businesses receive large volumes of cash or paper transactions that need to be paid into a bank. Many businesses pay these sums directly into their principal lending bank through the bank's branch network. This may be costly, inefficient and not strategically useful from a financial perspective.

A large wholesale company distributed goods throughout the UK using a network of distribution centres and trucks. When depositing the goods with a customer the truck driver was expected to collect either cash or cheques. The driver was trained to complete a deposit slip towards the end of each day and then find a bank branch and pay the money in.

One problem with doing this was that there were few bank branches in certain parts of the UK. This could result in time delays and security issues. Another problem was that the bank did not like receiving cash and imposed a cash-handling charge of 75p per cent (that is, 75p for every €100 of cash deposited). Given the billions of turnover that this company collected, this charge was considerable. Another issue was that the bank had a large degree of control over the customer's financial arrangements and could exercise considerable control – not good strategic financial management for a borrower!

The solution was to pay the cash and cheques into a transmission bank using Post Office Counters. This had many advantages. For a start the Post Office had more than five times as many branches as the wholesaler's bank, and they were often in locations outside a town centre where parking was easier. The Post Office actually needed cash, and the value of this was reflected in the overall charge to the wholesaler, thereby reducing its bank charges. The transmission bank made a single daily transfer by CHAPS for the total value of funds paid into the transmission account by the wholesaler. This meant that the wholesaler eliminated most of the fee from the principal bank and replaced this with just the single CHAPS fee and the transmission bank's fee, which was much lower, having been partially offset by the cash credit value from the Post Office.

It is always worth exploring alternative schemes to reduce bank fees. However, another important benefit earned by this wholesaler was independence from its principal bank. By using a transmission bank for deposits, it could at any time issue an instruction to have the value of the funds transferred to any other bank offering favourable facilities.

Case 6: Credit ratings and fundamental analysis

Icelanders recently voted not to repay the £3bn owed to Britain and the Netherlands following the crash of the country's banking system in 2008. Britain and the Netherlands compensated their nationals who lost savings deposited with Icesave accounts owned by Landisbanki, which collapsed in 2008.

Deposits made to failed Icelandic banks included those from individual citizens and also 127 English local authorities holding English public funds. It is one thing for an individual to make a bad investment but another for a professional treasurer at a local authority to risk public funds.

Understanding risk and whether one is authorized to take one is a key factor worth examining here. A treasurer handling public money has a prime responsibility to protect it. Is s/he empowered to take anything other than the lowest-risk investment available? How many authorities continued to make investments of public money after the credit ratings of the collapsed Icelandic banks were reduced?

So, we have public treasurers making bad investments with public money entrusted to them and Iceland not standing behind its debt. One way or another the public lose out, either through their direct investments or through their money being invested on their behalf by public authorities.

What lessons have we learned from this and how will these affect our future investment decisions? What this has reminded us is:

- Don't ignore fundamental analysis.
- Don't assume that a big name is a sound investment if the fundamentals don't stack up.
- Don't ignore credit ratings.
- Don't just follow others – they may be heading for the rocks.
- Do understand your risks.
- Assume that when things go wrong it may take years for you to get some of your money back and that you might never get any of it back in you lifetime.

A business cannot afford to ignore these basic principles – there are few government or taxpayer hand-outs to a business. Theses principles do not just apply to investments but also to any other judgements regarding the financial status of organizations you are dealing with. How reliable are they and will they pay your bill?

The market value of a company may often exceed its fundamental value. There are many things that influence market values other than pure asset values and earnings. Sentiment, emotion and general market conditions to name a few. However, a wise financial manager will understand fundamental values and know by how much these may vary from market values. This can then be considered as part of the risk analysis.

Case 7: Advantages and disadvantages of internal charging

This case concerns a medium-sized, not-for-profit organization with a turnover of around $400m per annum. It was jointly owned by a number of institutions that enjoyed an economy of scale in sharing a resource. It provided a good service and, compared with the alternative of each parent company owning its own resource, the not-for-profit organization was competitive. This was periodically checked by comparing charge-out rates with those offered in the outsourcing market.

Although the organization was on the face of it competitive, its costs and resources crept up each year and its owners/customers questioned whether there was scope for efficiencies. Naturally, each departmental head wanted to provide the best and most professional service and in so doing often justified additional resources.

To address the concerns about increasing costs, the first step taken was to introduce a form of ZBB (zero-based budgeting) whereby all departmental budgets had to demonstrate how they related to corporate goals. This helped to an extent but still additional resource was justified across the board, and, perhaps some managers were to some extent competing for power and influence by having the greatest resources under their control.

In a further attempt to control costs a system of internal charging was introduced. This system required every department to identify its customers (these were mainly internal customers) and to charge these customers for the service it provided. The internal customer had the choice of using the internal provider or finding an external one. Each internal department had to balance its books, in that the income it received from its customers had to be at least equal to its costs.

Departments first of all needed to identify their services and the resources used in providing them. For example, one service provided by the HR department was recruitment. This included assisting with job descriptions, advertising and interviewing. A charge would be advised to potential internal customers for this service. The customer could either accept this charge or use an external recruitment agency.

The supporters of this system argued that it would make managers act like businessmen and run a professional service. They also argued that it would make users aware of the costs of services they used. It was even possible that the service provided internally could also be provided externally if it met return on capital requirements and was in the remit of the organization's core business activity. This could bring in extra income to the organization and make the core service provided to the owners/customers even less expensive.

The sceptics argued that it would be too difficult to identify an internal customer. For example, who is the internal departmental customer for the annual report and accounts and taxation return completed by the finance department? The sceptics also argued that the system would just introduce another layer of administration with internal invoices and recording.

The new system was implemented, and during the budget preparation stage each budget holder would seek agreement from identified internal customers to pay for services. A department that did not have sufficient income would need to explain why, and a decision could be made as to whether to continue with the service internally or to outsource or to scrap the service altogether. The result was an overall reduction in costs. However, management attention was to some extent diverted from pure service provision to running a mini-business and the sceptics felt that service levels had deteriorated. A particular problem occurred when some departments wanted to use a particular internal service and others did not. If the costs of the internal services in question were fixed or difficult to reduce, then a decision would need to be made as to whether the whole service should be outsourced. Sceptics would argue that too much outsourcing would make the organization vulnerable.

In the end it was only those services that could be readily outsourced that were subject to internal charging; these were:

- payroll;
- HR;
- accounts receivable and payable;
- IT support services;
- catering;
- printing;
- legal services;
- security;
- premises management.

In theory internal charging systems help management in not-for-profit organizations to control and redistribute funds. However, many argue that there is no evidence that it really helps make better management decisions. It is a debate that has been ongoing for many years and, if you work in the public sector, I am sure you will have your own well-developed views.

Case 8: Marginal costing v full absorption costing

A director of the business banking arm of a major bank was reviewing the profitability of a portfolio of customers. The management accountant had produced the following statement showing the profitability of the account during the year ended 2010:

Business deposits made over the counter	€35,500,000
Fees at 4 cents per €100 of deposits	€14,200
Variable direct counter costs	€7,000
Gross margin	€7,200 (51%)
Fixed overheads allocated	€8,000
Net loss	€800

The director requested that the fees be increased from 4 cents to 4.5 cents per €100 of deposits in order to return the account to profitability. The customer refused to pay the increase and the director let the customer leave to join another bank. The director thought he had just got rid of a loss of €800 and was rather pleased with himself. In fact he had just lost the bank €7,200.

What he had done was to lose €14,200 of fee income and also €7,000 of variable costs. This resulted in a loss of the gross margin of €7,200. However, he did not lose the fixed overheads of €8,000!

He had simply lost €7,200 of contribution towards the fixed costs of €8,000 that remained regardless of his action. So, unless he could replace the lost business with more profitable business (which he had not) he had reduced the bank's bottom line.

Now, this might seem obvious to you but it is amazing how many senior executives struggle with this simple concept and lose their organizations' money.

Of course, not all accounts can be run on a marginal cost basis. Overall, fixed costs must be covered. However, consider whether you will be worse off by losing contribution before letting an account go.

Case 9: Overtrading: profits but no cash

A small regional advertising agency specialized for many years in buying space in local papers and selling it to small businesses that wanted to place advertisements. In a way it performed a service of aggregation and of dealing with large volumes of enquiries. For this service it made a small margin, employed several people and provided its shareholders with a small return on their investment. It also added value and income through some low-level design work and copy work. There was little financial risk and the company had, by and large, operated on 30-days' credit. It was allowed 30 days to pay invoices received from the newspapers and allowed some of its own customers 30 days. Most small customers paid as they ordered an advertisement and accordingly the agency was generally in funds. It had a small overdraft facility but rarely needed to use it.

The directors decided to find new income streams. Their existing business was coming under threat as more people placed advertisements directly with publishers online. They decided that the agency needed to provide more services and increase the value of their offerings. They would protect and develop their existing customer base, and attract new customers by offering web design, copywriting, marketing strategy, branding, PR and other services. Their ambition was to become a full service agency.

The company had not in the past needed a finance director and had simply used a bookkeeping service and a firm of local accountants to prepare and file year-end accounts. A finance director was the last thing on their minds at first and they quickly recruited very able people to undertake the work and an experienced business developer. Things got off to a good start and in no time at all orders for work were flowing into the agency.

The work commanded good rates and the margins were much higher than had previously been earned on buying space in local newspapers and selling on. The directors produced management reports that showed high levels of sales and profits. On the basis of this the company took on more orders and recruited more staff. There was no shortage of work and profits.

However, the company started to run into cash-flow problems because, although it had a full order book and was charging out at a high margin, there was a delay in collecting debts. Customers were slow to pay and were taking on average between 60 and 90 days credit. This lag did not match the agency's outgoings, which were 30 days. The new staff and premises were a regular monthly cash outflow.

The company was trading profitably but it was trading beyond its cash resources. It was overtrading. It could not pay its debts as they fell due and collapsed. It had left it too late to go to the bank and arrange facilities. The bank now just saw a company unable to pay its staff and rent, and was not about to jump in and save the day since it had no assurance on the quality and ability of the agency's customers to pay the debts. The company sacked most of its staff and started again in a restructured and better-financed manner.

You would have heard the saying that sales are vanity, profits are sanity but cash is king. Well it is not a bad thing to remember. Over-trading is a common cause of collapse of profitable companies.

Case 10: Integrating the planning and budgeting process, leading to outsourcing

This case concerns a large service provider that enables organizations with high volumes of business transactions to outsource their documentation handling and data-processing. The company receives batches of prime-source documents from customers and processes these at a number of regional centres. It also provides an outsourcing service for the processing of electronic transactions.

The company had been operating profitably in the 20 years since it had commenced trading with a small team supporting the founders. It had now grown to an organization employing around 1,100 employees with all of the support functions needed. These support functions had been built up by departmental heads who prepared their annual budgets in isolation from the main corporate planning process. The central business plan was prepared by the original executive team, most of whom had been with the organization since inception. Their principal concerns were the core processes surrounding the business offerings, and with winning and retaining new customers. Specialist support functions such as HR, payroll, buying, finance, premises management and training had been left to functional heads.

The company now found that it was employing nearly as many support staff as it was direct processing and sales staff. Business support costs were now more than half of the company's total costs and it was finding that its return on capital was being eroded. The executive team started to examine the support departments' budgets, which had been prepared on a resource basis. This meant, for example, that they could see what the money was being spent on but they could not see how this related to the company's overall business strategy or value-creating activities. For example, they could see that HR was budgeting for 25 staff and 15 weeks of staff training, but how did this relate to core business activities and was it really all necessary? People in HR were extremely busy. Similar questions surrounded all other support departments. They were all very professional and hard working, but were they really all needed? Market pressures were making the retention of customers and winning new ones extremely difficult at the prices that would provide the margins now needed to cover indirect overheads. Clearly something needed to be done!

As is often the case when things get to this stage, the executive team need a quick fix. They need to cut costs now in order to remain competitive and this would be painful and difficult. What costs could be cut without harming essential support, and what effect would all this have on company morale? Before we consider the options that this company considered and eventually adopted, let's look at some of the events that let to this situation and how the company could have prevented it from happening in the first place.

The founding team were all experts in the field that was the company's core competence. They would be the first to admit that they had little expertise in the other professional services they required. As a consequence they hired professionals and let them manage their own functions, largely in isolation. The support professionals did this and, while it would not be fair to say that they built empires, they each wanted their department to provide the best possible service. The company provided an outsourced service for other organizations that recognized its services was not their core competence. However, the team had neglected to recognize this fundamental themselves. As a consequence much of the company's resource was used in areas where they might not be as efficient as other providers, and where they certainly did not enjoy the economy of scale that they would if they outsourced some of their internal services.

The business plan was prepared each year showing how the company's offering would be developed, the demand, competition and expected market share at certain price levels. This was converted into an operations plan and sales plan. Budgets were simply prepared on a resource basis of last year's spend plus an allowance for inflation and business growth. This was the root of the problem. The company should have used a more rigorous method of budgeting to ensure that budgets supported the business plan at each stage. They might have expected managers to accept the business plans and goals, and then start with a blank sheet and estimate the resources they needed to support each item in the plan. A form of zero-based budgeting (ZBB) might have been beneficial. The principal point here is that planning and budgeting should be integrated. A fully integrated planning and budgeting system will help ensure that departmental budgets are aligned with business plans and that resources are justified in terms of the core business.

The company decided to adopt a two-stage approach to the problem. First of all they would introduce a fully integrated planning and budgeting system, and then they would consider outsourcing some of their support services. They wanted to get back to concentrating on their core business.

The first stage in the planning and budgeting process was to consider the business environment, including customers and competition, and prepare objectives, goals, key tasks and an overarching strategy. This was translated into sales and operations plans and budgets. These master plans and budgets were then given to the support departments, who were required to form their own plans and budgets to support the master sales and production requirements. These were prepared on a ZBB basis, with the requirement that each item had to be justified. This obviously made departmental managers think a bit harder than they had done before when simply preparing resource budgets, and some tough questions were asked at budget review time. Overall, the company achieved a modest reduction in support costs that, although welcome, was not enough to ensure the company could be competitive. However, plans and budgets were now integrated, and by relating support department overheads to overall corporate sales and production plans it was possible to more accurately determine product costs. In time the company adopted a form of activity-based costing and started to get a firmer grip on costs.

The second stage of the solution to cutting high support costs was to consider outsourcing those services that were not areas of core competence. Having already got costs under some control, the company thought it had a better understanding of how to approach discussions with various outsourcing and shared-services organizations. An initial idea was to move a whole department into specialist-service company that would take over all existing staff. The specialist-service company would offer a small reduction in cost but, more importantly, offered to hold costs for a number of years and meet service levels that were in excess of those currently being achieved by the internal resource. The outsourcing company would achieve this through an economy of scale that would be achieved through natural staff departures over time. Their current staff turnover would accommodate this, and staff being taken on would be assured of employment on either existing work or work for other clients. A bonus to the staff being transferred was that by working for a company that specialized in their profession they would learn new skills, be more marketable and have greater job security. This was all possible and financially viable now that the company had got its support costs under control and had made some initial internal savings.

The company is now trading successfully with a much smaller core team focusing on their area of core competence.

Shared services and outsourcing are simply an efficient business architecture that creates sustainable business advantage through the pooling of shared resources. The main benefits of outsourcing and shared services are cost reduction, performance improvement and the ability to leverage investments in new technology.

There are many types of shared service and outsourcing options, and in this case the company decided upon full outsourcing of certain support services to third-party suppliers once it had implemented an integrated planning and budgeting system and reduced costs as far as it practically could.

Case 11: Government deficits and cost cutting

For many generations the United States has been the economic power house of the world. Now, according to the Congressional Budget Office, the federal government will accumulate more than $7 trillion in new debt by 2019 unless remedial action is taken. The International Monetary Fund has estimated that the annual structural deficit in the United States may reach $1 trillion by 2015 under current policies.

A fiscal imbalance of these proportions is a risk to the United States since an accumulation of debt of this magnitude will lead to inflation and undermine currency stability, and will also adversely affect the private sector's ability to create wealth and jobs. The federal government has recognized that it needs to adopt an aggressive plan to reduce and ultimately eliminate the deficit. The Office of Management and Budget has, therefore, already commenced a programme to identify cost reductions.

The situation in the UK is similar although of a smaller scale, and cost cutting and efficiency measures are high on the government's agenda.

Of course the books have to balance; few would disagree with this fundamental. Much debate, however, concerns the severity of the cuts and how they can be spread so as to avoid doing more damage to the economy.

In the UK benefit entitlement and the elimination of some less essential programmes are the first to attract attention. Then all departments are expected to identify efficiencies and to cut back on spending and recruitment. Opportunities for the amalgamation and consolidation of services and departments and, in particular, for shared services are some of the more obvious initiatives. There are, no doubt, opportunities for efficiencies in energy consumption, supply chains and more straight-through transaction processing.

Reading this case there are obvious similarities with the previous case, Number 10. Similar actions are being taken. The question is what planning and budgetary measures can be put in place to prevent past mistakes happening again.

Clearly it is necessary to ensure that budgets support plans and objectives and that there is adequate funding for public expenditure. The problem is often the definition of the objective, since many programmes have broad social outcomes. Unclear outcomes make the evaluation of benefits difficult to measure.

Following the global financial crisis, many countries are struggling to emerge from low economic growth and high unemployment. Countries are in debt and also wondering how to cope with huge budget deficits. There is a possibility of long-term pain. Many still look to the United States to lead the world into a new period of economic prosperity, and perhaps new technological innovation will enable this. However, it has often been said that if companies managed their finances the way that governments do, they would be out of business in weeks.

How does the UK government manage its finances? Not at all well, according to the National Audit Office! A National Audit Office report on improving financial management in government concluded that Whitehall departments needed to improve financial management and accounting skills. It said that government departments were weak at monitoring balance sheets and cash flow.

Case 12: A 5 per cent increase in sales is generally worth more than a 5 per cent reduction in costs

A national retail company gave its store managers a certain amount of autonomy regarding stock, price and costs. The rationale behind this was that local managers had a better understanding of local needs.

At one store in the South of England a new manager was appointed who had been with the company since leaving school. She had worked her way up the ranks from counter-assistant to supervisor and, following a period with head office in buying, was now promoted to be manager of a medium-sized store.

Having worked in most departments she knew most of the 'tricks of the trade' and was keen to show how she could improve branch profitability.

The results for the 12 months prior to her taking up the post were:

Sales	£3,000,000
Gross profit	£1,650,000 (55 per cent)
Store wages & overheads	£700,000
Net profit	£950,000

Her experience had made her aware of some staff inefficiencies, and also of various practices regarding returns that might have benefited staff but not the company's bottom line. She resolved to increase the net profit by 5 per cent and determined to do this through cutting local costs and increasing efficiency.

Staff turnover was running at about 20 per cent per annum, and an early decision was simply not to replace leaving staff and to get the remaining workforce to cover the work by rearranging their duties. Another move was to stop the long-established practice of staff purchasing returns at concessionary rates. Generally staff practices were tightened up and costs were cut wherever possible.

At the end of the first 12 months the new manager had reduced local costs by the 5 per cent she had intended. Gross margins had remained the same. Sales had dipped by just 3 per cent. She thought this was a fair result until her regional manager called her in to explain why her store's net profit had fallen by 1.5 per cent.

The results were:

	This year	Previous year	Variance (%)
Sales (£)	2,910,000	3,000,000	3% adverse
Gross profit (£)	1,600,500 (55%)	1,650,000 (55 per cent)	
Store wages & overheads	£665,000	700,000	5% favourable
Net profit	£935,500	950,000	1.5% adverse

What is clear from these results is that a variance of sales has a greater effect on the bottom line than a variance on costs. A 3 per cent reduction in sales more than offset a 5 per cent reduction in store costs, resulting in an overall reduction in net profit.

For example, a 5 per cent increase in sales would have added £150,000 straight onto the bottom line, whereas a 5 per cent reduction in store costs would only add £35,000 to the bottom line.

This is not to say that reducing costs is not worthwhile; of course it is. However, it is a common mistake to focus too much on costs, perhaps because they are easier to control. Finding ways to get customers to spend more is not so controllable or easy. Many new managers, especially those who have come up though an operations' route, perhaps concentrate too much on cost because that is within their comfort zone and area of knowledge.

However, in this case questions also had to be asked about why sales had fallen by 3 per cent when elsewhere in the country sales had increased or at least remained level. Well, not replacing staff had meant that there were fewer sales staff to advise and promote sales. This may have had something to do with the reduced turnover. Perhaps the most critical factor was a palpable reduction in staff morale resulting from extra work loads and a reduction in perks. They had worked as a team and were not happy with the new manager's cost cutting and lack of encouragement of new ideas – it was all about control not new business. Unhappy staff can have a downward effect on customer spend. A smile can go a long way.

Case 13: Large capital projects and cost control: critical path analysis and integration with mainstream accounts

This case concerns the building of an oil platform and the owning oil company's capital budgeting techniques.

The original capital budget was based upon contractors' estimates consolidated and compiled by the oil company's consultant quantity surveyors and cost engineers. It came to around €80 million and the project duration was 36 months.

Half way into the project the costs had already reached nearly €200 million. Overruns were primarily due to delays in key activities that lay on the project's critical path. It had become exceedingly difficult to control costs and analyse variances because there were multiple contracts relating to multiple activities, and the task of reconciling financial records to the critical path analysis had become almost impossible. Costs were hopelessly out of control.

A new project manager and team were engaged and their first task was to prepare an estimate of the total cost to completion. To do this they first of all prepared a project network and critical path showing each activity's start, duration and completion date. The contracts relating to each activity were identified and coded, to ensure that accounts were integrated and all invoices were to be coded against an activity. The revised cost estimate was over €500 million.

By fully integrating the mainstream financial records with the project's activities and contracts it was now possible to monitor and control costs accurately. Previously the project software used, whilst recording contract costs against activities, had not been fully integrated with mainstream accounts and some transactions had slipped through the net, causing 'surprises' when finance produced high-level reports of the overall project cost. A key factor in controlling large projects is to determine just how sensitive the project costs are to slippage of an activity on the critical path. A relatively small and low-cost activity might, if it were delayed, cause slippage in major activities and result in a loss of a weather window or cause some other major disruption.

In summary, projects have activities and events. Contracts may cover more than one event. Ensure that the mainstream finance records are fully integrated with contract records and with the network/critical path. Watch out for those projects that lie on the critical path, however small they are, and see how sensitive the final outcome is to these critical activities. Understand the risks and take measures to hedge against them.

Case 14: A mass of figures just makes life more complicated

In this book we have discussed many techniques and ways of looking at business performance. The secret to good management information, of course, is knowing which figures to look at and act upon. This will be different for every type of business. Not knowing what is important and relevant will lead to over-complexity, confusion and generally missing the important point. Having too many figures will mean you can't see the woods for the trees.

The most successful companies concentrate on key performance figures – a dashboard approach. Digging deeper might be necessary but initial management attention needs to focus on key performance indicators.

Most of the unsuccessful companies I have observed have spent too long looking at micro-issues and as a consequence losing focus on what is important.

John Timpson is the Chief Executive of the high-street cobbler and key cutter Timpson. His group has over 800 shops. In an article in the *Daily Telegraph* Mr Timpson commented: 'A long time ago I learnt that having a lot of figures doesn't mean that you are better informed – it just makes life more complicated.' He went on to explain how having detailed figures for every shop took up management time just reviewing figures, with little end influence on performance. 'Sales never seemed to follow our forecast – our customers clearly didn't know how much they were expected to spend! I scrapped the process.' By not wasting time on unnecessary micro-management, Mr Timpson found that he had more time to know which shops are successful, to actually visit branches and pass the secrets of success around.

If you find that you are receiving management information that seems to take up much of your time but to have little effect on the performance of your business, then there is a good chance that you are concentrating on the wrong things. One of the biggest dangers in any business is 'doing the wrong thing really well'.

Case 15: High levels of fixed costs when income is variable can cause failure

We have discussed the difference between fixed costs (those that remain fixed when sales or production increases) and variable costs (those that change with sales or production activity).

A company that has a high proportion of its costs fixed during a period of time when it cannot be sure of sales income for the same period is extremely vulnerable. It has a 'mis-match' between fixed costs and variable income, so that if sales fall it will be left with costs it cannot afford to cover. It may go broke very quickly.

In June 2011 the case of Southern Cross in the UK demonstrated this basic trap that organizations often fall foul of. That is having overheads that are fixed or rising at a time when revenues are under pressure to remain constant or fall. Southern Cross had rented property at a fixed or increasing level at a time when its income was constrained.

Many companies assume that their sales forecasts will be achieved but unless they have contracts in place to back up the forecasts, they should consider what might happen if income falls. Can their costs fall at the same rate? A company that has entered into a property rental for a fixed period will need to be pretty sure that its income during the same period is certain. If not then it is taking a gamble.

There is no doubt that during the next few months the causes for the Southern Cross failure will be debated in the press, and certainly by the time you read this book the case will be dead and buried. Blame will have been laid in many directions and the case will have become so confusing that only those who have followed it closely will understand the real reasons behind the failure. However, a key risk measurement is the ratio of fixed costs to assured income during a period and you might consider, as I do, that this was a major contributing factor in the failure.

As another real example, a group of independent schools has the following simple way of keeping tabs on its fixed cost: assured income ratio.

£ millions	Years 2011–2013		
	Costs (£)	Income (£)	Surplus (£)
Fixed/contracted	1.4	0.4	
Variable/to be contracted	17.6	20.2	
Totals	19.0	20.6	1.6

During the three-year period most of the schools' income is considered as uncommitted since parents are only required to pay one term in advance. However, most of the schools' costs are also variable in the same period because staff can be reduced if student numbers fall. The group of schools do have some real fixed costs during the three-year period, and it tries to ensure that these are partially covered by parents paying for fees in advance and uses the balance by cash reserves to cover the mis-match.

If the schools did not keep adequate cash reserves, then the mis-match between fixed costs of £1.4m and contracted income of £0.4m would put them at risk if student numbers fell sharply. Independent schools are regularly closing down when student numbers fall at a time when they are saddled with a high proportion of fixed or rising maintenance costs. For schools in this category the difference between success and failure can amount to just a few students.

Many new start-up companies that do not have significant cash resources will ensure that their costs are mainly variable. As a director of a company, you have a responsibility to ensure that the company does not incur a debt at a time when it is unable to ensure it can repay it. You might want to consider this carefully when matching the company's ability to cover costs with revenue during a particular period!

Case 16: Interest rates and inflation

Let's conclude our case studies with a debate on interest rates and inflation, with some examples of the effect of government policy on the use of interest rates to stem inflation and how this might affect your own business.

In the UK we have for several years experienced the lowest bank rate in my lifetime, and that is a very long time! Inflation has also been very low but at the time of writing it has started to creep up again.

Successive chancellors and governments have seen interest-rate targets as a vital tool of monetary policy to fight inflation. A general theory espoused by some chancellors is that when inflation increases one should increase interest rates to choke it off. Nowadays the Monetary Policy Committee (MPC) is responsible for interest-rate setting and has the difficult task of setting a rate that will achieve an optimal balance between the necessary fight against inflation and very many other economic factors. It is indeed a difficult task and not all members will agree on the same course of action.

Sometimes a member of the MPC will speak outside the committee at a public meeting, expressing a personal view on interest rates. This might be simple 'kite flying' or just a deeply held view. It might be an indication of future movements but then it might not! So, how do interest rates affect inflation and how does inflation affect interest rates? How do interest rates affect rates of currency exchange? More importantly for your business, how will this all affect you?

Lower interest rates might create more borrowing power for consumers. This might enable consumers to spend more, resulting in economic growth and possibly creating inflation. When the MPC, the Fed or some similar policy committee decides that the economy is growing so fast that demand might outpace supply and increase inflation, it might decide to increase interest rates as a way of slowing down the amount of cash entering the economy. This might reduce inflation in the longer term.

Similarly, increasing inflation might increase interest rates. This is because real money supply is money supply divided by price level. This means that as prices increase the money available will decrease, and a decrease in money supply would result in higher interest rates.

Unfortunately, things do not always obey popular economic belief. I can remember one British Chancellor announcing monthly increases in interest rates in the belief that inflation would 'give in'. Interest rates reached an all-time high and this had the effect of closing down many businesses, thereby reducing certain supplies and increasing prices in some areas. This partially offset the effect that the increased interest rates had on reducing consumer spending, which was expected to bring down inflation. Interest rates are also a component of most product costs, so that increasing rates can increase costs. Whilst interest rates had reached an all-time high the pound had become a desirable investment for many overseas investors. This created demand for Sterling and strengthened the pound to such an extent that exporters found it difficult to sustain overseas sales. One can go on with this debate. The point is that setting a correct interest rate is hard and can become very political. Interest rates can take a long time to have an effect on inflation but can have a very quick effect on business survival, especially for new businesses and those with a high level of borrowing.

So, how will all this affect your business and what can you do about it? Some companies like to hedge against changes in interest rates in order to secure rates that are manageable to their business. Other companies like to go with the market. All companies should have a policy that lays down how interest rate fluctuations should be recognized and managed. To do this, it is necessary to model for your company different scenarios under different interest rates, inflation rates and exchange rates. See how sensitive your results are to these variables and then decide how you can cover this risk.

One cash-rich international oil company prepared a scenario analysis for a major new capital investment. It found that interest rate increases resulted in:

- little immediate effect on its cost of borrowing;
- a greater return on cash invested;
- a reduction in the price of imported product, resulting from a strengthening of the pound;
- longer-term cost savings resulting from lower inflationary pressures;
- higher return expectations from shareholders;
- little immediate effect on the price of its product in the UK, which was linked to global commodity prices.

At the same time a medium-sized, mainly bank-funded, manufacturing company that exported its product found that the increases in interest rates resulted in:

- a large increase in its cost of borrowing;
- reduced export sales and margins because of the stronger pound;
- longer-term cost savings resulting from lower inflationary pressures;
- higher return expectations from shareholders.

The manufacturing company collapsed, thereby reducing the value of the UK's export sales.

The conclusion that you might draw from this is that rather than just going with the market you should prepare a full business-risk and scenario analysis and take advance measures to protect your business in the short to medium term from the immediate effect of longer-term policies of a government.

APPENDIX 1

Discounted cash flow tables

Years	Rate of discount given to 3 decimal places														
	1	2	3	4	5	6	7	8	9	10	11	12	13	14	15
1	990	980	971	962	952	943	935	926	917	909	901	893	885	877	870
2	980	961	943	925	907	890	873	857	842	826	812	797	783	769	756
3	971	942	915	889	864	840	816	794	772	751	731	712	693	675	658
4	961	924	888	855	823	792	763	735	708	683	659	636	613	592	572
5	951	906	863	822	784	747	713	681	650	621	593	567	543	519	497
6	942	888	837	790	746	705	667	630	596	564	535	507	480	456	432
7	933	871	813	760	711	665	623	583	547	513	482	452	425	400	376
8	923	853	789	731	677	627	582	540	502	467	434	404	376	351	327
9	914	837	766	703	645	592	544	500	460	424	391	361	333	308	284
10	905	820	744	676	614	558	508	463	422	386	352	322	295	270	247
11	896	804	722	650	585	527	475	429	388	350	317	287	261	237	215
12	887	788	701	625	557	497	444	397	356	319	286	257	231	208	187
13	879	773	681	601	530	469	415	368	326	290	258	229	204	182	163
14	870	758	661	577	505	442	388	340	299	263	232	205	181	160	141
15	861	743	642	555	481	417	362	315	275	239	209	183	160	140	123
16	853	728	623	534	458	394	339	292	252	218	188	163	141	123	107
17	844	714	605	513	436	371	317	270	231	198	170	146	125	108	93
															30

Discount factors are given to 3 decimal places with the decimal point omitted.

Formulae: $\frac{1}{(1+i)^n}$ where i = rate of discount and n = number of years

Use the above formulae if you need to extend the table's rows or columns

Example of use: The value of £1 in 5 years' time using the discount factor is 3% or 86p.

APPENDIX 2

Compound interest tables

Years (n)	Interest rates 1%	2%	3%	4%	5%	6%	7%	8%
1	1.01	1.02	1.03	1.04	1.05	1.06	1.07	1.08
2	1.02	1.04	1.061	1.082	1.102	1.124	1.145	1.166
3	1.03	1.061	1.093	1.125	1.158	1.191	1.225	1.26
4	1.041	1.082	1.126	1.167	1.216	1.262	1.311	1.36
5	1.051	1.104	1.159	1.217	1.276	1.338	1.404	1.469
6	1.061	1.126	1.194	1.265	1.34	1.419	1.501	1.587
7	1.072	1.149	1.23	1.316	1.407	1.504	1.606	1.714
8	1.083	1.172	1.267	1.369	1.477	1.594	1.718	1.851
9	1.094	1.195	1.306	1.423	1.551	1.689	1.838	1.999
10	1.105	1.219	1.344	1.48	1.629	1.791	1.967	2.159

INDEX

(italics indicate a figure or table in the text)